Vulkan Expert: Mastering High-Performance Graphics

Vulcan Fundamentals

Kameron Hussain and Frahaan Hussain

Published by Sonar Publishing, 2023.

While every precaution has been taken in the preparation of this book, the publisher assumes no responsibility for errors or omissions, or for damages resulting from the use of the information contained herein.

VULKAN EXPERT: MASTERING HIGH-PERFORMANCE GRAPHICS

Table of Contents

Chapter 1: Optimization Fundamentals

Section 1.1: Profiling Your Vulkan Application

CPU Profiling

GPU Profiling

Section 1.2: Bottleneck Analysis

Profiling Tools

GPU Timing Queries

CPU Profiling

Section 1.3: GPU and CPU Synchronization Optimization

Pipeline Barriers

Multithreading and Command Buffer Submission

Resource Buffering

Section 1.4: Batch Rendering Techniques

What Is Batch Rendering?

Static Batching

Dynamic Batching

Frustum Culling and Occlusion Culling

Section 1.5: Reducing State Changes

State Change Overhead

Pipeline Layouts and Descriptor Sets

Object Sorting

Dynamic Uniform Buffers and Push Constants

Chapter 2: Advanced GPU Techniques

Section 2.1: Compute Shaders in Depth

What Are Compute Shaders?

Use Cases for Compute Shaders

Writing Compute Shaders

Dispatching Compute Shaders

Section 2.2: GPGPU (General Purpose GPU) Programming

Introduction to GPGPU

GPGPU Frameworks and Libraries

Writing GPGPU Kernels

Integrating GPGPU with Vulkan

Performance Considerations

Section 2.3: Direct Memory Access and Persistence

Understanding DMA

Vulkan Memory Types

Mapping Memory

Memory Persistence

Section 2.4: Multi-GPU Programming

Benefits of Multi-GPU Programming

Challenges of Multi-GPU Programming

Vulkan and Multi-GPU

Multi-GPU Rendering Techniques

Implementing Multi-GPU in Vulkan

Section 2.5: GPU Culling and LOD Optimization

GPU Culling

Level of Detail (LOD) Optimization

Implementing GPU Culling and LOD Optimization in Vulkan

Chapter 3: Complex Shader Techniques

Section 3.1: Shader Interpolation Methods

Understanding Shader Interpolation

Linear Interpolation (LERP)

Barycentric Coordinates

Perspective Correct Interpolation

Section 3.2: Stochastic Shading

Understanding Stochastic Shading

Applications of Stochastic Shading

Implementing Stochastic Shading in Vulkan

Section 3.3: Real-time Ray Tracing

Understanding Real-time Ray Tracing

Implementing Real-time Ray Tracing in Vulkan

Section 3.4: Subsurface Scattering Implementation

Understanding Subsurface Scattering

Implementing Subsurface Scattering in Vulkan

Section 3.5: Real-time Global Illumination Techniques

Understanding Real-time Global Illumination

Implementing Real-time Global Illumination in Vulkan

Chapter 4: Deep Learning in Graphics

Section 4.1: Neural Networks for Procedural Content

Procedural Content Generation (PCG)

Neural Networks in PCG

Advantages of Neural Networks in PCG

Challenges and Considerations

Section 4.2: Style Transfer in Real-time Rendering

Understanding Style Transfer

Applications of Style Transfer in Real-time Rendering

Implementing Style Transfer in Vulkan

Section 4.3: AI-driven Animation

Understanding AI-driven Animation

Significance of AI-driven Animation

Implementing AI-driven Animation in Vulkan

Section 4.4: Neural Networks in Texture Generation

Understanding Neural Networks in Texture Generation

Advantages of Neural Networks in Texture Generation

Implementing Neural Networks in Texture Generation with Vulkan

Section 4.5: Advanced AI for Game Logic

Understanding Advanced AI for Game Logic

Significance of Advanced AI in Gaming

Implementing Advanced AI in Vulkan-Based Games

Chapter 5: Advanced Simulation Techniques

Section 5.1: Fluid and Gas Dynamics

Understanding Fluid and Gas Dynamics Simulation

Applications of Fluid and Gas Dynamics Simulation

Numerical Methods for Fluid Simulation

Implementing Fluid Simulation in Vulkan

Section 5.2: Rigid Body Dynamics

Understanding Rigid Body Dynamics

Applications of Rigid Body Dynamics

Numerical Methods for Rigid Body Dynamics

Implementing Rigid Body Dynamics in Vulkan

Section 5.3: Soft Body Simulation with Finite Elements

Understanding Soft Body Simulation with Finite Elements

Applications of Soft Body Simulation

Numerical Methods for Soft Body Simulation

Implementing Soft Body Simulation in Vulkan

Section 5.4: Hair and Fur Simulation

Understanding Hair and Fur Simulation

Applications of Hair and Fur Simulation

Numerical Methods for Hair and Fur Simulation

Implementing Hair and Fur Simulation in Vulkan

Section 5.5: Crowd Dynamics

Understanding Crowd Dynamics Simulation

Applications of Crowd Dynamics Simulation

Numerical Methods for Crowd Dynamics Simulation

Implementing Crowd Dynamics Simulation in Vulkan

Chapter 6: Volumetric and Holographic Rendering

Section 6.1: Introduction to Volumetrics

Understanding Volumetric Rendering

Applications of Volumetric Rendering

Implementing Volumetric Rendering in Vulkan

Section 6.2: Real-time Volumetric Shadows

Understanding Volumetric Shadows

Techniques for Real-time Volumetric Shadows

Implementing Real-time Volumetric Shadows in Vulkan

Section 6.3: Holographic Displays and Vulkan

Understanding Holographic Displays

Challenges in Rendering for Holographic Displays

Implementing Holographic Rendering in Vulkan

Section 6.4: Holographic Shader Techniques

Simulating Light Field Synthesis

Handling Parallax

Realistic Materials and Lighting

Special Effects and Interaction

Performance Optimization

Section 6.5: Interactive Volumetric Data Visualization

Understanding Volumetric Data

Techniques for Interactive Volumetric Data Visualization

Implementing Interactive Volumetric Visualization in Vulkan

Chapter 7: Advanced Real-time Ray Tracing

Section 7.1: Implementing Path Tracing

Understanding Path Tracing

Implementing Path Tracing in Vulkan

Section 7.2: Photon Mapping

Understanding Photon Mapping

Implementing Photon Mapping in Vulkan

Section 7.3: Radiance and Irradiance Caching

Understanding Radiance and Irradiance Caching

Implementing Radiance and Irradiance Caching in Vulkan

Section 7.4: Real-time Caustics

Understanding Caustics

Implementing Real-time Caustics in Vulkan

Section 7.5: Noise Reduction Techniques

Understanding Image Noise

Noise Reduction Techniques

Chapter 8: Realistic Atmospheric and Weather Effects

Section 8.1: Atmospheric Scattering

The Physics of Atmospheric Scattering

Implementing Atmospheric Scattering

Section 8.2: Real-time Cloud Simulation

Challenges in Cloud Simulation

Techniques for Real-time Cloud Simulation

Section 8.3: Dynamic Weather Systems

Importance of Dynamic Weather

Implementing Dynamic Weather

Section 8.4: Natural Phenomena (e.g., Rainbows, Aurora)

Simulating Rainbows

Simulating Auroras

Section 8.5: Earth and Space Rendering Techniques

Earth Rendering Techniques

Space Rendering Techniques

Chapter 9: Hardware and Driver Deep Dive

Section 9.1: Understanding Graphics Hardware Architecture

Parallel Processing Units:

Memory Hierarchy:

Shader Execution:

Pipelines and Stages:

Graphics APIs:

Profiling and Analysis:

Section 9.2: Driver Internals and Optimization

The Role of Graphics Drivers:

Command Buffer Generation:

Resource Management:

Synchronization and Multithreading:

Driver Overhead:

Profiling and Debugging:

Driver Updates:

Section 9.3: Hardware Tessellation Techniques

Understanding Tessellation:

Tessellation Control Shader (TCS):

Tessellation Evaluation Shader (TES):

Primitive Assembly:

Tessellation Factors:

Practical Applications:

Performance Considerations:

Tessellation Culling:

Section 9.4: Low-level GPU Programming

Advantages of Low-level GPU Programming:

Challenges of Low-level GPU Programming:

Vulkan API for Low-level GPU Programming:

Use Cases for Low-level GPU Programming:

Section 9.5: Future of Graphics Hardware

Ray Tracing Acceleration:

AI and Machine Learning Integration:

Quantum Computing Impact:

Real-time Hardware-accelerated Physics:

Customizable Graphics Pipelines:

Increased Integration of Graphics and Compute:

Energy Efficiency and Sustainability:

Chapter 10: Immersive Audio Techniques

Section 10.1: Binaural and 3D Audio

Understanding Binaural Audio:

3D Audio Spatialization:

Section 10.2: Real-time Reverberation Techniques

Understanding Reverberation:

Techniques for Real-time Reverberation:

Integration with Graphics:

Conclusion:

Section 10.3: Advanced Audio Simulation

Modeling Sound Propagation:

Dynamic Environmental Effects:

Ambisonics and Spatial Audio:

Integration with Graphics:

Conclusion:

Section 10.4: Sound Propagation in Complex Environments

Reflection and Reverberation:

Occlusion and Diffraction:

Real-Time Updates:

Integration with Graphics:

Section 10.5: Audio Shaders and Processing

Audio Shaders:

Real-time Audio Processing:

Integration with Graphics:

Spatial Audio:

Dynamic Audio Environments:

Chapter 11: Procedural Generation Techniques

Section 11.1: Procedural Modelling and Texturing

Section 11.2: Infinite Worlds and Fractal Geometry

Section 11.3: Real-time Ray Tracing

Section 11.4: Subsurface Scattering Implementation

The Physics of Subsurface Scattering

Implementation Steps

Section 11.5: Dynamic Story and World Generation

The Concept of Dynamic Generation

Techniques for Dynamic World Generation

Challenges and Considerations

Examples of Dynamic Generation

Chapter 12: Mixed Reality Rendering

Section 12.1: Merging VR and AR Techniques

Understanding Mixed Reality

Combining VR and AR Technologies

Applications of MR

Challenges and Future Trends

Section 12.2: Real-time Object Tracking

Tracking Technologies

Challenges in Object Tracking

Use Cases for Object Tracking in MR

Future Trends

Section 12.3: Scene Reconstruction from Video

Techniques for Scene Reconstruction

Applications of Scene Reconstruction in MR

Challenges and Future Directions

Section 12.4: Real-world Lighting in AR

Challenges in Real-world Lighting

Techniques for Real-world Lighting in AR

Hardware Considerations

Future Directions

Section 12.5: Physical and Virtual Interactions

The Challenge of Interactions

Techniques for Physical and Virtual Interactions

Hardware Considerations

Future Developments

Chapter 13: Optical and Visual Effects

Section 13.1: Understanding Human Visual System

The Human Eye Anatomy

Visual Perception

Visual Illusions and Perceptual Phenomena

Visual Fatigue and Comfort

Applying Knowledge to Graphics

Section 13.2: Optical Illusions in Graphics

1. Müller-Lyer Illusion

2. Ponzo Illusion

3. Kanizsa Triangle

4. Checker Shadow Illusion

5. Motion Illusions

Section 13.3: Physiological Effects in Graphics

1. High Dynamic Range (HDR)

2. Color Blindness

3. Flicker Sensitivity

4. Virtual Reality (VR) and Motion Sickness

5. Eye Strain and Fatigue

Section 13.4: Adaptive Rendering Techniques

1. Dynamic Resolution Scaling

2. Level of Detail (LOD) Adjustment

3. Texture Streaming and Loading

4. Quality Presets and User Preferences

5. Environmental and Runtime Factors

Section 13.5: Future of Display Technologies

1. Foldable and Rollable Displays

2. Augmented Reality (AR) Glasses

3. 3D Holographic Displays

4. Advanced Materials for Displays

5. Eye-tracking and Biometric Feedback

6. Energy-efficient Displays

Chapter 14: Advanced Networking and Cloud Integration

Section 14.1: Cloud-rendered Graphics

1. On-demand Scalability

2. Cross-platform Compatibility

3. Reduced Latency Challenges

4. Data Security and Privacy

5. Cost Management

6. Real-time Streaming and Compression

Section 14.2: Real-time Stream Decomposition

1. Understanding Stream Decomposition

2. Use Cases in Cloud-rendered Graphics

3. Considerations for Implementation

4. Real-world Applications

Section 14.3: Multiplayer VR and AR Systems

1. Networking for Multiplayer VR and AR

2. User Interaction and Collaboration

3. Challenges and Solutions

4. Applications and Impact

Section 14.4: Server-side Physics and Logic

1. Importance of Server-side Physics and Logic

2. Challenges in Server-side Implementation

3. Techniques for Server-side Physics and Logic

4. Applications and Impact

Section 14.5: Scalable Game Servers and Microservices

1. The Need for Scalability

2. Microservices Architecture

3. Common Microservices in Games

4. Scalability Challenges

5. Impact on Game Development

Chapter 15: Security and Anti-cheat Mechanisms

Section 15.1: Understanding Common Exploits

Exploits vs. Cheating

Wallhacks and Aimbots

Speed Hacks

Exploiting Bugs and Glitches

DDoS Attacks

Prevention and Detection

Section 15.2: Secure OpenGL Programming

Input Validation

Shader Security

Memory Safety

Shader Compilation and Linking

Resource Management

Section 15.3: Anti-cheat Techniques and Mechanisms

Client-Side Anti-Cheat Measures

Server-Side Anti-Cheat Mechanisms

Reporting and Community Involvement

Continuous Improvement

Section 15.4: Encrypted Networking in Games

The Need for Encrypted Networking

Implementing Encryption Protocols

Public Key Infrastructure (PKI)

Challenges and Considerations

Conclusion

Section 15.5: Forensics and Post-breach Analysis

The Importance of Post-breach Analysis

Incident Response Plan

Digital Forensics

Learning from Incidents

Conclusion

Chapter 16: Toolchain and Workflow Mastery

Section 16.1: Advanced Debugging Techniques

Profiling and Performance Analysis

Real-time Debugging

Memory Analysis

Integration with Graphics Debugging Tools

Collaborative Debugging

Continuous Integration (CI)

Live Coding and Hot Reloading

Code and Asset Pipelining

Conclusion

Section 16.2: Continuous Integration for Graphics Projects

The Basics of Continuous Integration

Benefits of CI in Graphics Development

Setting Up CI for Graphics Projects

Example CI Configuration (Travis CI)

Monitoring and Notifications

Conclusion

Section 16.3: Shader and Asset Pipelining

The Significance of Shader and Asset Pipelining

Key Components of a Shader and Asset Pipeline

Implementing a Shader and Asset Pipeline

Benefits of a Robust Pipeline

Section 16.4: Live Coding and Hot Reloading

What is Live Coding?

The Benefits of Live Coding

Implementing Live Coding

Challenges of Live Coding

Section 16.5: Collaborative Tools and Techniques

Version Control Systems (VCS)

Integrated Development Environments (IDEs)

Collaboration Platforms

Cloud-Based Services

Collaborative Development Practices

Collaborative Graphics Workflows

Challenges of Collaboration

Chapter 17: Integrating Emerging Technologies

Section 17.1: Quantum Computing and Graphics

Understanding Quantum Computing

Potential Applications in Graphics

Challenges and Limitations

Quantum Computing Tools for Graphics

Future Outlook

Section 17.2: Integrating Biometrics in Games

Understanding Biometrics in Gaming

Potential Applications

Benefits of Biometric Integration

Considerations and Challenges

Tools and Technologies

Future of Biometrics in Gaming

Section 17.3: Brain-computer Interfaces

Understanding Brain-computer Interfaces

Applications in Gaming

Benefits of BCI Integration

Challenges and Considerations

Tools and Technologies

Future Outlook

Section 17.4: Graphics for Advanced Robotics

Simulation and Training

Human-Robot Interaction

Control and Visualization

Challenges and Considerations

Tools and Technologies

Future Directions

Section 17.5: Evolution of Wearable Tech

Historical Perspective

Rise of Smartwatches

Augmented Reality (AR) and Virtual Reality (VR)

Healthcare and Biometrics

Fashion and Lifestyle

Future Trends

Chapter 18: Open Standards and Future Graphics APIs

Section 18.1: Beyond OpenGL: Vulkan and DirectX

The Legacy of OpenGL

The Emergence of Vulkan

DirectX: Microsoft's Graphics API

Choosing the Right API

Section 18.2: Open Standards in the Graphics World

The Importance of Open Standards

Khronos Group: Driving Open Standards

WebGL: Bringing 3D Graphics to the Web

The Role of OpenXR in VR/AR

Cross-API Techniques and Tools

The Future Landscape

Section 18.3: The Evolution of Web Graphics

Early Web Graphics

The Emergence of Flash

The Rise of HTML5 and Canvas

WebGL: Bringing 3D Graphics to the Browser

WebGPU: The Next Frontier

Real-time Ray Tracing on the Web

The Role of WebAssembly

Progressive Web Apps (PWAs)

Conclusion

Section 18.4: Cross-API Techniques and Tools

Abstraction Layers

Graphics Middleware

Low-Level API Wrappers

Cross-API Debugging and Profiling

Compatibility Testing

Code Generation and Abstraction

Conclusion

Section 18.5: The Future Landscape of Graphics Programming

Real-time Ray Tracing

AI and Machine Learning Integration

Quantum Computing

Web-Based Graphics

AR and VR Integration

Cross-Platform Development

Sustainability and Energy Efficiency

Inclusivity and Accessibility

Conclusion

Chapter 19: Ethics, Accessibility, and Inclusion

Section 19.1: Designing for All Users

User-Centered Design

Inclusive User Interfaces

Color Considerations

Responsive Design

Accessibility Standards

Consider Cognitive Accessibility

Testing and Feedback

Legal Compliance

Conclusion

Section 19.2: Addressing Photosensitive Epilepsy Concerns

Understanding Photosensitive Epilepsy

Avoiding Flashing Lights

Flicker-Free Animation

Testing and Compliance

User Options

Informative Warnings

Educating Designers and Developers

Monitoring and Updates

Legal Requirements

Conclusion

Section 19.3: Ethical Considerations in Graphics Technology

1. Representation and Diversity

2. Privacy and Data Security

3. Environmental Impact

4. Digital Rights Management (DRM) and Licensing

5. Algorithmic Bias and Fairness

6. Social and Cultural Sensitivity

7. User Well-being

8. Transparency and Accountability

Section 19.4: Open Source and Community Contributions

1. Collaborative Development

2. Accessibility

3. Customization and Flexibility

4. Learning and Skill Development

5. Community Support

6. Building a Portfolio

7. Contributions to Libraries and Tools

8. Code Quality and Review

9. License and Legal Considerations

10. Documentation and Communication

11. Contributing Beyond Code

12. Recognizing Diversity

13. Sustainability

Section 19.5: Ensuring Future Tech is Inclusive

1. Accessibility Matters

2. User-Centered Design

3. Designing for Diversity

4. Addressing Photosensitive Epilepsy Concerns

5. Ethical Considerations

6. Inclusive Design Tools

7. Education and Awareness

8. User Testing

9. Inclusive Development Teams

10. Internationalization and Localization

11. Community Engagement

12. Feedback Mechanisms

13. Advocacy for Inclusivity

Chapter 20: Final Project: Building a Graphics Tech Demo

Section 20.1: Brainstorming Cutting-edge Ideas

Section 20.2: Integrating Multiple Advanced Techniques

Choosing the Right Techniques

Implementing Techniques

Creating a Cohesive Experience

Section 20.3: Design Considerations for Modern Hardware

Leveraging the Latest Hardware Features

Scalability and Accessibility

Real-time Monitoring and Feedback

Future-Proofing Your Demo

Embracing Emerging Trends

Section 20.4: Presentation and Showcasing

Creating a Captivating Trailer

Demos and Playable Teasers

Online Presence

Events and Conventions

Feedback and Iteration

Accessibility

Collaboration and Networking

Section 20.5: Reflections and Future Exploration

Reflecting on Achievements

Lessons Learned

Future Exploration

Setting New Goals

Chapter 1: Optimization Fundamentals

Section 1.1: Profiling Your Vulkan Application

Profiling is a crucial step in optimizing your Vulkan application. It involves gathering performance data to identify bottlenecks and areas for improvement. In this section, we will explore various profiling techniques and tools to help you analyze and optimize your Vulkan application.

Profiling can be broadly categorized into two types: CPU profiling and GPU profiling. CPU profiling focuses on understanding the CPU-side performance of your application, while GPU profiling delves into the performance of the graphics card.

CPU Profiling

CPU PROFILING HELPS you identify CPU-bound operations and bottlenecks in your Vulkan application. One commonly used tool for CPU profiling is Intel VTune Profiler[1], which provides detailed insights into CPU usage and helps pinpoint performance bottlenecks.

To use VTune Profiler, you can instrument your Vulkan code with markers and collect performance data during execution. Here's an example of how to instrument your code with markers:

// Include the VTune header

```
#include <ittnotify.h>
```

---

1. https://software.intel.com/content/www/us/en/develop/tools/vtune-profiler.html

```
// ...

// Create a VTune domain

__itt_domain*                    vtune_domain                    =
__itt_domain_create("VulkanProfiling");

// Start a VTune frame

__itt_frame_begin_v3(vtune_domain, NULL);

// Your Vulkan rendering code goes here

// End the VTune frame

__itt_frame_end_v3(vtune_domain, NULL);
```

Once you've instrumented your code, you can run your application with VTune Profiler attached to gather CPU profiling data.

GPU Profiling

GPU PROFILING FOCUSES on understanding how the GPU is utilized by your Vulkan application. Vulkan provides a set of profiling queries[2] that allow you to measure GPU performance metrics such as GPU time, pipeline statistics, and memory usage.

Here's an example of how to use Vulkan's timestamp queries to measure GPU time:

```
// Create a query pool for timestamp queries

VkQueryPoolCreateInfo queryPoolInfo = {};

queryPoolInfo.sType                                              =
VK_STRUCTURE_TYPE_QUERY_POOL_CREATE_INFO;
```

---

2. https://www.khronos.org/registry/vulkan/specs/1.2/html/chap45.html

```
queryPoolInfo.queryType = VK_QUERY_TYPE_TIMESTAMP;

queryPoolInfo.queryCount = 2; // Create two queries for start and
end timestamps

VkQueryPool queryPool;

vkCreateQueryPool(device, &queryPoolInfo, nullptr,
&queryPool);

// Record timestamp queries in your command buffer

vkCmdWriteTimestamp(commandBuffer,
VK_PIPELINE_STAGE_BOTTOM_OF_PIPE_BIT, queryPool,
0);

// ... Vulkan rendering commands ...

vkCmdWriteTimestamp(commandBuffer,
VK_PIPELINE_STAGE_BOTTOM_OF_PIPE_BIT, queryPool,
1);

// Retrieve query results after executing the command buffer

uint64_t timestamps[2];

vkGetQueryPoolResults(device, queryPool, 0, 2, sizeof(uint64_t) *
2, timestamps, 0, VK_QUERY_RESULT_64_BIT);
```

Profiling your Vulkan application using both CPU and GPU profiling techniques is essential for optimizing its performance. In the upcoming sections of this chapter, we will dive deeper into bottleneck analysis, GPU and CPU synchronization optimization, batch rendering techniques, and reducing state changes to further enhance the performance of your Vulkan application.

Section 1.2: Bottleneck Analysis

BOTTLENECK ANALYSIS is a crucial step in the optimization process of your Vulkan application. Identifying bottlenecks allows you to focus your optimization efforts on the areas that will have the most significant impact on performance. In this section, we will delve into various techniques and tools for bottleneck analysis in Vulkan applications.

Profiling Tools

TO PERFORM BOTTLENECK analysis effectively, you'll need to leverage profiling tools. These tools provide insights into where your application spends the most time during execution. One widely used profiling tool for Vulkan is RenderDoc[3], which allows you to capture frames, inspect GPU workloads, and identify performance bottlenecks.

Using RenderDoc, you can capture frames from your Vulkan application and analyze them to pinpoint performance bottlenecks. It provides a detailed timeline view that visualizes how your GPU resources are utilized over time.

GPU Timing Queries

VULKAN PROVIDES GPU timing queries, which are valuable for identifying GPU-related bottlenecks. Timing queries allow you to measure the time taken by specific GPU operations, such as rendering a frame or executing a compute shader. These queries can be used to profile specific parts of your rendering pipeline.

Here's an example of how to use Vulkan timing queries to measure the GPU time for rendering a frame:

---

3. https://renderdoc.org/

```cpp
// Create a query pool for timestamp queries
VkQueryPoolCreateInfo queryPoolInfo = {};

queryPoolInfo.sType                                      =
VK_STRUCTURE_TYPE_QUERY_POOL_CREATE_INFO;

queryPoolInfo.queryType = VK_QUERY_TYPE_TIMESTAMP;

queryPoolInfo.queryCount = 2; // Create two queries for start and
end timestamps

VkQueryPool queryPool;

vkCreateQueryPool(device,        &queryPoolInfo,        nullptr,
&queryPool);

// Begin a query

vkCmdWriteTimestamp(commandBuffer,
VK_PIPELINE_STAGE_BOTTOM_OF_PIPE_BIT, queryPool,
0);

// ... Vulkan rendering commands ...

// End the query

vkCmdWriteTimestamp(commandBuffer,
VK_PIPELINE_STAGE_BOTTOM_OF_PIPE_BIT, queryPool,
1);

// Retrieve query results after submitting the command buffer

uint64_t timestamps[2];

vkGetQueryPoolResults(device, queryPool, 0, 2, sizeof(uint64_t) *
2, timestamps, 0, VK_QUERY_RESULT_64_BIT);
```

// Calculate the GPU time for rendering the frame

```
uint64_t gpuTime = timestamps[1] - timestamps[0];
```

By measuring the GPU time for different parts of your rendering process, you can identify which components contribute the most to the overall frame time, helping you focus your optimization efforts.

CPU Profiling

WHILE GPU PROFILING is essential, don't forget to profile the CPU side of your application as well. CPU bottlenecks can have a significant impact on overall performance. Profiling tools like Intel VTune Profiler can help you identify CPU bottlenecks and hotspots in your code.

In summary, bottleneck analysis is a critical step in optimizing Vulkan applications. Profiling tools, GPU timing queries, and CPU profiling can help you identify and address performance bottlenecks effectively. In the following sections of this chapter, we will explore GPU and CPU synchronization optimization, batch rendering techniques, and strategies for reducing state changes to further enhance the performance of your Vulkan application.

Section 1.3: GPU and CPU Synchronization Optimization

EFFICIENT SYNCHRONIZATION between the GPU and CPU is essential for maximizing the performance of your Vulkan application. In this section, we will explore techniques and best practices for optimizing synchronization between these two crucial components of your graphics pipeline.

Pipeline Barriers

PIPELINE BARRIERS IN Vulkan are used to synchronize access to resources, ensuring that data is read and written in the correct order. Using pipeline barriers efficiently can minimize unnecessary synchronization overhead. You can use pipeline barriers to transition images and buffers between different layouts and access types.

Here's an example of using a pipeline barrier to transition an image from a color attachment to a shader read-only layout:

```
VkImageMemoryBarrier barrier = {};

barrier.sType                                            =
VK_STRUCTURE_TYPE_IMAGE_MEMORY_BARRIER;

barrier.oldLayout                                        =
VK_IMAGE_LAYOUT_COLOR_ATTACHMENT_OPTIMAL;

barrier.newLayout                                        =
VK_IMAGE_LAYOUT_SHADER_READ_ONLY_OPTIMAL;

barrier.srcQueueFamilyIndex                              =
VK_QUEUE_FAMILY_IGNORED;

barrier.dstQueueFamilyIndex                              =
VK_QUEUE_FAMILY_IGNORED;

barrier.image = image; // The image to transition

barrier.subresourceRange.aspectMask                      =
VK_IMAGE_ASPECT_COLOR_BIT;

barrier.subresourceRange.baseMipLevel = 0;

barrier.subresourceRange.levelCount = 1;
```

```
barrier.subresourceRange.baseArrayLayer = 0;

barrier.subresourceRange.layerCount = 1;

barrier.srcAccessMask                    =
VK_ACCESS_COLOR_ATTACHMENT_WRITE_BIT;

barrier.dstAccessMask = VK_ACCESS_SHADER_READ_BIT;

vkCmdPipelineBarrier(

commandBuffer,

VK_PIPELINE_STAGE_COLOR_ATTACHMENT_OUTPUT_BIT,

VK_PIPELINE_STAGE_FRAGMENT_SHADER_BIT,

0,

0, nullptr,

0, nullptr,

1, &barrier

);
```

It's essential to use pipeline barriers only when necessary to avoid unnecessary synchronization. Overusing barriers can lead to performance degradation.

Multithreading and Command Buffer Submission

UTILIZING MULTITHREADING can significantly improve the CPU's ability to generate command buffers and submit work to the GPU. Vulkan allows you to create multiple threads for generating command buffers concurrently, which can be particularly beneficial for applications with a complex rendering pipeline.

When using multithreading, it's crucial to synchronize the submission of command buffers to the GPU to avoid data races and ensure correct rendering order. Vulkan provides mechanisms like semaphores and fences to achieve this synchronization.

Resource Buffering

RESOURCE BUFFERING involves managing multiple copies of resources to avoid synchronization stalls between the CPU and GPU. For example, double or triple buffering techniques can be applied to avoid the GPU waiting for the CPU to finish rendering a frame.

Resource buffering can be implemented for various types of resources, such as uniform buffers, vertex buffers, and images. Properly managing these resource buffers can help maintain a steady flow of work to the GPU.

In conclusion, optimizing GPU and CPU synchronization is crucial for achieving high performance in Vulkan applications. Efficient use of pipeline barriers, multithreading, and resource buffering are key techniques to minimize synchronization overhead and maximize GPU utilization. In the following sections of this chapter, we will explore batch rendering techniques and strategies for reducing state changes to further enhance Vulkan application performance.

Section 1.4: Batch Rendering Techniques

BATCH RENDERING TECHNIQUES are essential for optimizing Vulkan applications, as they can significantly reduce the overhead of submitting draw calls to the GPU. In this section, we will explore various batch rendering strategies and best practices to improve the rendering performance of your Vulkan application.

What Is Batch Rendering?

BATCH RENDERING INVOLVES grouping multiple objects or primitives into a single draw call, reducing the number of API calls and command buffer submissions. By rendering objects in batches, you can minimize CPU overhead and GPU driver overhead associated with draw calls.

Static Batching

STATIC BATCHING IS suitable for objects that do not change frequently or remain constant throughout a frame. In Vulkan, you can use techniques like instanced rendering and indirect drawing to efficiently render multiple instances of the same object with a single draw call.

Here's a simplified example of using instanced rendering to render multiple instances of an object:

// Create a buffer containing instance data

VkBuffer instanceBuffer;

// Fill instanceBuffer with per-instance data

// Create a descriptor set with the instance buffer

VkDescriptorSet descriptorSet;

// Update descriptor set with instanceBuffer

// Bind descriptor set and use instanced rendering

vkCmdBindDescriptorSets(commandBuffer, VK_PIPELINE_BIND_POINT_GRAPHICS, pipelineLayout, 0, 1, &descriptorSet, 0, **nullptr**);

```
vkCmdBindPipeline(commandBuffer,
VK_PIPELINE_BIND_POINT_GRAPHICS, graphicsPipeline);

vkCmdDrawIndexed(commandBuffer,                    indexCount,
instanceCount, firstIndex, 0, 0);
```

By using instanced rendering, you can efficiently render a large number of instances with minimal CPU overhead.

Dynamic Batching

DYNAMIC BATCHING IS suitable for objects that change frequently or have different properties, such as materials or transformations, within a single frame. To implement dynamic batching, you can organize objects with similar properties into batches and use dynamic uniform buffers or push constants to update per-object data efficiently.

Here's a simplified example of dynamic batching with dynamic uniform buffers:

```
// Create a dynamic uniform buffer

VkBuffer dynamicUniformBuffer;

// Fill dynamicUniformBuffer with per-object data for a batch

// Bind dynamic uniform buffer and use dynamic batching

vkCmdBindDescriptorSets(commandBuffer,
VK_PIPELINE_BIND_POINT_GRAPHICS, pipelineLayout, 0,
1, &descriptorSet, 0, nullptr);

vkCmdBindPipeline(commandBuffer,
VK_PIPELINE_BIND_POINT_GRAPHICS, graphicsPipeline);
```

```
vkCmdBindDescriptorSets(commandBuffer,
VK_PIPELINE_BIND_POINT_GRAPHICS, pipelineLayout, 1,
1, &dynamicUniformBuffer, 0, nullptr);

vkCmdDrawIndexed(commandBuffer,                    indexCount,
instanceCount, firstIndex, 0, 0);
```

Dynamic batching allows you to efficiently handle objects with varying properties without incurring significant CPU overhead.

Frustum Culling and Occlusion Culling

TO FURTHER OPTIMIZE batch rendering, consider implementing frustum culling and occlusion culling techniques. Frustum culling involves discarding objects that are outside the camera's view frustum, while occlusion culling avoids rendering objects that are occluded by others.

By incorporating these techniques into your Vulkan application, you can reduce the number of objects processed and submitted for rendering, improving both CPU and GPU performance.

In summary, batch rendering techniques are crucial for optimizing Vulkan applications. Static batching, dynamic batching, and culling methods can significantly reduce CPU overhead and improve rendering performance. In the following sections of this chapter, we will explore strategies for reducing state changes to further enhance Vulkan application performance.

Section 1.5: Reducing State Changes

EFFICIENTLY MANAGING state changes in your Vulkan application is crucial for optimizing rendering performance. Unnecessary state changes can lead to increased CPU overhead and GPU driver overhead. In this section, we will explore strategies and best practices for minimizing state changes in your Vulkan application.

State Change Overhead

STATE CHANGES IN VULKAN involve modifying various pipeline states, such as shaders, render passes, and descriptor sets, to prepare the GPU for rendering different objects or materials. Each state change can incur a significant performance cost due to validation and pipeline reconfiguration.

To minimize this overhead, it's essential to organize your rendering pipeline in a way that reduces the frequency of state changes.

Pipeline Layouts and Descriptor Sets

PIPELINE LAYOUTS DEFINE the interface between your shaders and the resources they access. Vulkan allows you to create multiple pipeline layouts, each optimized for a specific set of shaders and resources. By using appropriate pipeline layouts, you can reduce the number of descriptor set bindings and pipeline state changes.

Here's an example of how to create and use pipeline layouts efficiently:

```
// Create pipeline layout for static objects

VkPipelineLayoutCreateInfo layoutInfo = {};

// Configure layoutInfo with appropriate descriptor set layouts and push constant ranges

VkPipelineLayout staticPipelineLayout;

vkCreatePipelineLayout(device, &layoutInfo, nullptr, &staticPipelineLayout);
```

```
// Create pipeline layout for dynamic objects

VkPipelineLayout dynamicPipelineLayout;

// Create a separate layout for dynamic objects

// Bind the appropriate pipeline layout before rendering

vkCmdBindPipelineLayout(commandBuffer,
VK_PIPELINE_BIND_POINT_GRAPHICS,
staticPipelineLayout);

// Bind descriptor sets and push constants

// Render static objects

// Switch to the dynamic pipeline layout

vkCmdBindPipelineLayout(commandBuffer,
VK_PIPELINE_BIND_POINT_GRAPHICS,
dynamicPipelineLayout);

// Bind descriptor sets and push constants

// Render dynamic objects
```

By using separate pipeline layouts for different object types or materials, you can minimize unnecessary pipeline state changes.

Object Sorting

SORTING OBJECTS OR primitives by their material properties or shaders can help reduce state changes. Grouping objects with the same rendering requirements together allows you to minimize descriptor set and pipeline layout changes.

Consider implementing a sorting mechanism that organizes objects based on their rendering characteristics before rendering the frame.

Dynamic Uniform Buffers and Push Constants

INSTEAD OF CREATING separate uniform buffers for every object, consider using dynamic uniform buffers or push constants for per-object data. Dynamic uniform buffers allow you to update a portion of a buffer with new data for each object, reducing the number of buffer bindings and state changes.

Here's a simplified example of using dynamic uniform buffers:

```
// Create a dynamic uniform buffer

VkBuffer dynamicUniformBuffer;

// Fill dynamicUniformBuffer with per-object data for a batch

// Bind dynamic uniform buffer and use dynamic batching

vkCmdBindDescriptorSets(commandBuffer,
VK_PIPELINE_BIND_POINT_GRAPHICS, pipelineLayout, 0,
1, &descriptorSet, 0, nullptr);

vkCmdBindPipeline(commandBuffer,
VK_PIPELINE_BIND_POINT_GRAPHICS, graphicsPipeline);

vkCmdBindDescriptorSets(commandBuffer,
VK_PIPELINE_BIND_POINT_GRAPHICS, pipelineLayout, 1,
1, &dynamicUniformBuffer, 0, nullptr);

vkCmdDrawIndexed(commandBuffer,                    indexCount,
instanceCount, firstIndex, 0, 0);
```

Dynamic uniform buffers and push constants can significantly reduce state changes related to per-object data.

In summary, minimizing state changes is crucial for optimizing Vulkan application performance. Efficiently managing pipeline layouts, sorting objects, and using dynamic uniform buffers or push constants are key strategies to reduce CPU and GPU overhead associated with state changes. In the following chapters, we will explore more advanced optimization techniques to further enhance your Vulkan applications.

Chapter 2: Advanced GPU Techniques

Section 2.1: Compute Shaders in Depth

Compute shaders are a powerful feature of modern graphics APIs like Vulkan, allowing for highly parallelized data processing tasks on the GPU. In this section, we will delve into compute shaders, exploring their capabilities, use cases, and how to leverage them effectively in your Vulkan applications.

What Are Compute Shaders?

COMPUTE SHADERS ARE a type of shader program specifically designed for general-purpose computing tasks. Unlike vertex and fragment shaders, which are primarily used for rendering, compute shaders are not bound to the rendering pipeline. Instead, they provide a flexible way to perform computations on the GPU.

Use Cases for Compute Shaders

COMPUTE SHADERS HAVE a wide range of use cases, making them a versatile tool for GPU programming. Some common use cases include:

1. Image Processing

- Compute shaders can efficiently process images, performing operations like filtering, blurring, and edge detection.

2. Physics Simulations

- Compute shaders are ideal for physics simulations, including particle systems, fluid dynamics, and cloth simulations.

3. Data Parallelism

- Tasks that involve processing large amounts of data in parallel can benefit from compute shaders. Examples include data sorting, compression, and cryptography.

4. Terrain Generation

- Generating complex terrains or procedural landscapes can be accelerated using compute shaders.

5. Post-processing Effects

- Compute shaders are commonly used for post-processing effects like bloom, depth of field, and ambient occlusion.

Writing Compute Shaders

COMPUTE SHADERS IN Vulkan are written in the GLSL (OpenGL Shading Language) or SPIR-V (Standard Portable Intermediate Representation). Here's a simple example of a compute shader in GLSL that performs element-wise addition on two arrays:

```
#version 450

layout(set = 0, binding = 0) buffer InputBuffer {
```

```glsl
float data[];

};

layout(set = 0, binding = 1) buffer OutputBuffer {

float result[];

};

void main() {

uint index = gl_GlobalInvocationID.x;

result[index] = data[index] + 1.0;

}
```

This compute shader takes two buffers as input and performs element-wise addition, storing the results in an output buffer. It utilizes the gl_GlobalInvocationID to determine the index for each invocation.

Dispatching Compute Shaders

IN VULKAN, YOU DISPATCH compute shaders using the vkCmdDispatch command within a command buffer. You specify the number of workgroups in each dimension to define the execution configuration.

```cpp
// Dispatch the compute shader

vkCmdBindPipeline(commandBuffer,
VK_PIPELINE_BIND_POINT_COMPUTE,
computePipeline);
```

```
vkCmdBindDescriptorSets(commandBuffer,
VK_PIPELINE_BIND_POINT_COMPUTE, pipelineLayout, 0,
1, &descriptorSet, 0, nullptr);
```

```
vkCmdDispatch(commandBuffer,                workgroupCountX,
workgroupCountY, workgroupCountZ);
```

It's important to design your compute shaders with parallelism in mind to fully utilize the GPU's capabilities.

In conclusion, compute shaders are a versatile tool for leveraging the parallel processing power of the GPU in Vulkan applications. They find applications in a wide range of tasks, from image processing to physics simulations. Understanding how to write and dispatch compute shaders effectively can greatly enhance the performance and capabilities of your Vulkan applications.

Section 2.2: GPGPU (General Purpose GPU) Programming

GENERAL PURPOSE GPU programming, often abbreviated as GPGPU, harnesses the computational power of modern GPUs for non-graphics tasks. While compute shaders, as discussed in the previous section, are a form of GPGPU, this section explores GPGPU programming in greater depth, emphasizing its broader applications and techniques within Vulkan.

Introduction to GPGPU

TRADITIONALLY, GPUS were primarily designed for rendering graphics, but they have evolved into massively parallel processors capable of handling a wide range of general-purpose computations. GPGPU programming allows developers to offload computationally intensive tasks to the GPU, accelerating applications in various domains such as scientific simulations, machine learning, and data processing.

GPGPU Frameworks and Libraries

TO EFFECTIVELY UTILIZE the GPU for general-purpose tasks, you can leverage GPGPU frameworks and libraries. Some popular options include:

- **CUDA**: NVIDIA's parallel computing platform and programming model that allows developers to use NVIDIA GPUs for GPGPU programming.

- **OpenCL**: A cross-platform framework for heterogeneous computing that supports GPGPU programming on a variety of GPU vendors, including AMD and Intel.

- **Vulkan Compute**: Vulkan itself provides robust support for GPGPU through compute shaders and associated features.

Writing GPGPU Kernels

GPGPU KERNELS ARE THE heart of GPGPU programming. Kernels are small, parallelizable functions that can be executed on the GPU. Writing efficient GPGPU kernels requires careful consideration of memory access patterns, data parallelism, and workload distribution.

Here's a simplified example of a GPGPU kernel in OpenCL that performs element-wise multiplication of two arrays:

```
__kernel void multiply(__global float* a, __global float* b, __global float* result, int length) {
```

```
int globalID = get_global_id(0);

if (globalID < length) {

result[globalID] = a[globalID] * b[globalID];

}

}
```

In this example, the multiply kernel takes two input arrays (a and b) and an output array (result). It calculates the element-wise product of a and b.

Integrating GPGPU with Vulkan

VULKAN AND GPGPU CAN be seamlessly integrated in your application. Vulkan provides compute shaders, which are ideal for GPGPU tasks. You can create a Vulkan compute pipeline and use it to execute GPGPU kernels.

Here's a high-level overview of the steps to integrate GPGPU with Vulkan:

1. **Create a Compute Pipeline**: Define a Vulkan compute pipeline that includes your GPGPU compute shader.
2. **Set up Buffers**: Create Vulkan buffers to hold input and output data for your GPGPU kernels.
3. **Dispatch Compute Work**: Use the vkCmdDispatch command to execute GPGPU kernels within Vulkan command buffers.
4. **Synchronize Data**: Ensure proper synchronization between Vulkan and GPGPU tasks, especially if you need to read the results of GPGPU computations on the CPU.

Performance Considerations

EFFICIENT MEMORY MANAGEMENT and data transfer between the CPU and GPU are critical for GPGPU performance. Minimizing data movement and optimizing memory access patterns can significantly impact GPGPU performance.

Additionally, workload distribution and load balancing play a crucial role in achieving high GPU utilization. Dividing the work evenly among GPU compute units and avoiding thread divergence can lead to better performance.

In summary, GPGPU programming extends the capabilities of GPUs beyond graphics rendering and can greatly accelerate a wide range of computational tasks. Vulkan provides the necessary features and flexibility to integrate GPGPU seamlessly into your application. When leveraging GPGPU, consider factors like memory management, workload distribution, and synchronization to optimize performance.

Section 2.3: Direct Memory Access and Persistence

DIRECT MEMORY ACCESS (DMA) and memory persistence are important concepts in GPU programming, enabling efficient data transfer between the CPU and GPU, as well as minimizing redundant data copying. In this section, we will explore DMA and memory persistence techniques within the context of Vulkan.

Understanding DMA

DMA IS A MECHANISM that allows peripherals or devices, such as GPUs, to access memory directly without involving the CPU. This capability is essential for efficiently transferring data between the CPU and GPU or between different regions of GPU memory. DMA can significantly reduce CPU involvement in data transfer operations, improving overall system performance.

Vulkan Memory Types

IN VULKAN, MEMORY ALLOCATION and management are explicit and flexible. Vulkan provides different memory types, each with specific properties, to suit various usage scenarios. Two important memory types related to DMA and memory persistence are:

1. **Device-Local Memory**: This memory type is typically used for GPU resources, such as textures and buffers. It offers high performance but is not directly mappable to the CPU.
2. **Host-Visible Memory**: Host-visible memory is accessible from both the CPU and GPU. It is suitable for data that needs frequent updates by the CPU.

Mapping Memory

TO ENABLE DIRECT CPU access to GPU memory, you can map host-visible memory regions. Mapping memory allows you to read and write data to the mapped region, similar to working with regular CPU memory.

Here's a simplified example of mapping and updating a buffer in Vulkan:

// Create a host-visible buffer

VkBufferCreateInfo bufferInfo = {};

// Initialize bufferInfo with appropriate parameters

```cpp
VkBuffer buffer;

vkCreateBuffer(device, &bufferInfo, nullptr, &buffer);

// Allocate memory for the buffer

VkMemoryRequirements memRequirements;

vkGetBufferMemoryRequirements(device, buffer, &memRequirements);

VkMemoryAllocateInfo allocInfo = {};

// Initialize allocInfo with memory type flags and size

VkDeviceMemory bufferMemory;

vkAllocateMemory(device, &allocInfo, nullptr, &bufferMemory);

// Bind the memory to the buffer

vkBindBufferMemory(device, buffer, bufferMemory, 0);

// Map the buffer memory for CPU access

void* data;

vkMapMemory(device, bufferMemory, 0, bufferInfo.size, 0, &data);

// Update the buffer data

memcpy(data, newData, dataSize);

// Unmap the memory when done

vkUnmapMemory(device, bufferMemory);
```

Mapping memory allows efficient data transfers between the CPU and GPU without the need for intermediate buffers or redundant copying.

Memory Persistence

MEMORY PERSISTENCE is an extension of the concept of mapped memory. With memory persistence, you can map memory once and keep it mapped throughout the application's lifetime. This is particularly useful when you have data that needs frequent updates by both the CPU and GPU.

Memory persistence can be achieved by creating host-visible memory with the VK_MEMORY_PROPERTY_HOST_CACHED_BIT property flag. This flag indicates that memory should be cached for both reading and writing by the CPU.

VkMemoryAllocateInfo allocInfo = {};

// Initialize allocInfo with memory type flags, size, and VK_MEMORY_PROPERTY_HOST_CACHED_BIT

VkDeviceMemory bufferMemory;

vkAllocateMemory(device, &allocInfo, **nullptr**, &bufferMemory);

// Map the memory once and keep it mapped

void* data;

vkMapMemory(device, bufferMemory, 0, bufferInfo.size, 0, &data);

// Data can be updated by both CPU and GPU without frequent mapping/unmapping

// Unmap the memory when it's no longer needed

vkUnmapMemory(device, bufferMemory);

Memory persistence can lead to significant performance improvements when dealing with frequently updated data.

In conclusion, DMA and memory persistence are essential techniques for efficient data transfer and management in Vulkan applications. Understanding memory types, mapping memory, and leveraging memory persistence can help you optimize data transfer operations between the CPU and GPU while minimizing CPU involvement.

Section 2.4: Multi-GPU Programming

MULTI-GPU PROGRAMMING, also known as GPU multi-instancing, is a technique that involves utilizing multiple GPUs in a single system to improve rendering performance. In this section, we will explore multi-GPU programming in the context of Vulkan, discussing its benefits, challenges, and how to implement it effectively.

Benefits of Multi-GPU Programming

MULTI-GPU SETUPS OFFER several advantages for graphics rendering:

1. **Increased Rendering Power**: By using multiple GPUs, you can significantly increase the computational power available for rendering, allowing for more complex scenes and higher frame rates.
2. **High-Resolution Rendering**: Multi-GPU configurations are commonly used for high-resolution rendering, such as 4K or 8K gaming, where the increased processing power is essential for maintaining smooth performance.

3. **VR and AR Applications**: Virtual reality (VR) and augmented reality (AR) applications often require high frame rates and low latency. Multi-GPU setups can help meet these demanding requirements.

Challenges of Multi-GPU Programming

WHILE MULTI-GPU PROGRAMMING offers advantages, it also presents challenges:

1. **Synchronization**: Coordinating multiple GPUs can be complex. Ensuring that each GPU processes its portion of the frame and synchronizing their outputs can be challenging.
2. **Load Balancing**: Distributing the rendering workload evenly among GPUs is critical. Load imbalance can lead to suboptimal performance.
3. **Resource Management**: Efficiently managing GPU resources, including memory, textures, and buffers, across multiple GPUs can be complex.

Vulkan and Multi-GPU

VULKAN PROVIDES ROBUST support for multi-GPU configurations, enabling developers to harness the power of multiple GPUs efficiently. Vulkan's approach to multi-GPU programming involves explicit control, giving developers fine-grained control over how rendering workloads are distributed and synchronized.

Multi-GPU Rendering Techniques

SEVERAL TECHNIQUES can be employed when implementing multi-GPU rendering in Vulkan:

Alternate Frame Rendering (AFR):

AFR INVOLVES ASSIGNING each GPU to render alternating frames. For example, GPU1 renders frame 1, GPU2 renders frame 2, and so on. This approach balances the workload but may introduce some frame latency.

Split-Frame Rendering:

IN SPLIT-FRAME RENDERING, each frame is divided into sections, and each GPU is responsible for rendering a portion of the frame. This approach minimizes frame latency but requires careful synchronization.

A-Sync Multi-GPU:

ASYNCHRONOUS MULTI-GPU techniques allow GPUs to work on different parts of a frame concurrently, reducing frame latency. Vulkan's explicit control over synchronization mechanisms makes this approach viable.

Implementing Multi-GPU in Vulkan

TO IMPLEMENT MULTI-GPU rendering in Vulkan, you typically follow these steps:

1. **Detect Available GPUs**: Use Vulkan to enumerate the available GPUs in the system.
2. **Create a Device for Each GPU**: Create a Vulkan logical device for each GPU, specifying the GPU you want to use.
3. **Distribute Rendering Workload**: Divide the rendering workload among the GPUs, ensuring that each GPU is responsible for a specific portion of the frame.

4. **Synchronize Outputs**: Implement synchronization mechanisms to ensure that the outputs from all GPUs are correctly combined to produce the final frame.
5. **Resource Management**: Carefully manage GPU resources to avoid conflicts and efficiently use memory and buffers.

```cpp
// Detect and enumerate available GPUs

uint32_t gpuCount;

vkEnumeratePhysicalDevices(instance, &gpuCount, nullptr);

std::vector<VkPhysicalDevice> gpus(gpuCount);

vkEnumeratePhysicalDevices(instance, &gpuCount, gpus.data());

// Create a logical device for each GPU

std::vector<VkDevice> devices;

for (const auto& gpu : gpus) {

VkDevice device = CreateDeviceForGPU(gpu);

devices.push_back(device);

}

// Distribute rendering workload and synchronize outputs

for (int frame = 0; frame < numFrames; ++frame) {

for (size_t i = 0; i < devices.size(); ++i) {

RenderFrame(devices[i], frame);

}

SynchronizeFrames(devices);
```

```
}
```

// Resource management and cleanup

Implementing multi-GPU rendering in Vulkan requires careful planning and synchronization, but it can provide substantial performance benefits for graphics-intensive applications.

In summary, multi-GPU programming in Vulkan allows developers to leverage the combined power of multiple GPUs for rendering tasks. While it offers performance advantages, it also presents synchronization and load balancing challenges. By following best practices and choosing the appropriate multi-GPU rendering technique, developers can maximize the benefits of multi-GPU setups in Vulkan applications.

Section 2.5: GPU Culling and LOD Optimization

GPU CULLING AND LEVEL of Detail (LOD) optimization are techniques that play a crucial role in improving the rendering performance of Vulkan applications. In this section, we will explore these techniques, their benefits, and how to implement them effectively.

GPU Culling

GPU CULLING IS A TECHNIQUE used to eliminate objects or parts of objects that are not visible in the current camera view. By culling objects that are outside the camera's frustum or occluded by other objects, you can reduce unnecessary rendering work and improve frame rates.

Frustum Culling

FRUSTUM CULLING INVOLVES testing whether objects are within the camera's view frustum, which is the portion of the scene that is visible to the camera. Objects entirely outside the frustum can be safely culled from rendering.

Occlusion Culling

OCCLUSION CULLING DETERMINES whether objects are hidden behind other objects and, therefore, not visible. It uses techniques like depth testing and occlusion queries to identify occluded objects and avoid rendering them.

Level of Detail (LOD) Optimization

LEVEL OF DETAIL (LOD) optimization is a technique that involves using different versions of an object or model with varying levels of detail based on their distance from the camera. LOD optimization aims to reduce the computational load by rendering simpler versions of objects that are far away and more detailed versions as they come closer to the camera.

LOD Models

FOR LOD OPTIMIZATION, you typically prepare multiple versions of an object, each with a different level of detail. These LOD models can be generated manually or using algorithms, and they represent the same object but with varying polygon counts or simplifications.

Transition Criteria

TO DETERMINE WHEN TO switch between LOD levels, you need transition criteria. These criteria can be based on factors like the distance from the camera, the object's screen size, or other heuristics. When an object meets the transition criteria, you switch to a different LOD model.

Implementing GPU Culling and LOD Optimization in Vulkan

IMPLEMENTING GPU CULLING and LOD optimization in Vulkan involves several steps:

1. **Frustum Culling**: You can implement frustum culling in your application by checking whether an object's bounding volume intersects with the camera's frustum. This check can be done in the vertex shader or using compute shaders, and culled objects are skipped during rendering.
2. **Occlusion Culling**: Occlusion culling requires rendering occluder objects into a depth buffer and then using occlusion queries or hardware occlusion query results to determine which objects are occluded. Occluded objects can be culled before rendering.
3. **LOD Management**: LOD optimization involves managing multiple LOD models for each object and dynamically selecting the appropriate LOD level based on distance or other criteria. You switch between LOD models by updating the object's vertex or tessellation shaders.

Here's a simplified example of LOD optimization in Vulkan:

```glsl
// Vertex Shader for LOD management

layout(location = 0) in vec3 inPosition;

out vec3 fragPosition;

void main() {
// Calculate distance from camera

float distance = length(inPosition - cameraPosition);

// Determine LOD level based on distance

int lodLevel = CalculateLODLevel(distance);

// Select appropriate LOD model

gl_Position = projection * view * lodModels[lodLevel] * vec4(inPosition, 1.0);

fragPosition = gl_Position.xyz;

}
```

In this example, the vertex shader calculates the distance from the camera and selects the LOD model based on that distance.

GPU culling and LOD optimization are essential techniques for improving the rendering performance of Vulkan applications, especially for scenes with many objects. Properly implemented, these techniques can lead to smoother frame rates and better overall performance.

Chapter 3: Complex Shader Techniques

Section 3.1: Shader Interpolation Methods

Shader interpolation methods are fundamental to the rendering process, as they determine how values are smoothly interpolated across the surface of 3D objects. In this section, we will explore various interpolation techniques used in shaders to achieve realistic lighting, shading, and visual effects in Vulkan.

Understanding Shader Interpolation

SHADER INTERPOLATION refers to the process of smoothly transitioning values (such as colors, normals, or texture coordinates) across the surface of a 3D object during rendering. This interpolation is crucial for simulating the appearance of curved and detailed surfaces in computer graphics.

In Vulkan and other modern graphics APIs, shaders are executed for each vertex and fragment of a 3D object. The values calculated in the vertex shader are interpolated across the primitive (e.g., triangle) and passed to the fragment shader, where they are used to determine the final pixel color.

Linear Interpolation (LERP)

LINEAR INTERPOLATION, often abbreviated as LERP, is the most basic form of interpolation used in shaders. It smoothly blends two values based on a parameter (usually denoted as "t") that varies from 0 to 1. The LERP function is commonly used for interpolating colors, positions, and texture coordinates.

```
vec3 Lerp(vec3 a, vec3 b, float t) {

return mix(a, b, t);

}
```

In this example, the mix function performs linear interpolation between vectors a and b based on the parameter t.

Barycentric Coordinates

BARYCENTRIC COORDINATES are used for interpolating values across a triangle. Each point inside a triangle can be represented as a combination of the triangle's vertices using barycentric coordinates. These coordinates are used to interpolate values across the triangle's surface.

```
vec3 Barycentric(vec3 p, vec3 a, vec3 b, vec3 c) {

vec3 v0 = b - a;

vec3 v1 = c - a;

vec3 v2 = p - a;

float d00 = dot(v0, v0);

float d01 = dot(v0, v1);

float d11 = dot(v1, v1);

float d20 = dot(v2, v0);

float d21 = dot(v2, v1);

float denom = d00 * d11 - d01 * d01;

float u = (d11 * d20 - d01 * d21) / denom;
```

```
float v = (d00 * d21 - d01 * d20) / denom;

float w = 1.0 - u - v;

return vec3(u, v, w);

}
```

In this shader function, given a point p and the vertices a, b, and c of a triangle, we calculate the barycentric coordinates u, v, and w of the point within the triangle.

Perspective Correct Interpolation

IN PERSPECTIVE PROJECTION, linear interpolation of values can result in visual artifacts. Perspective-correct interpolation adjusts the interpolated values to account for the varying depth across the primitive. This correction helps maintain the correct appearance of textures and shading.

```
vec2 PerspectiveCorrectInterpolation(vec3 barycentric, vec2 v0, vec2 v1, vec2 v2, float depth0, float depth1, float depth2) {

float wRecip = 1.0 / (barycentric.x / depth0 + barycentric.y / depth1 + barycentric.z / depth2);

return vec2(

(barycentric.x / depth0) * wRecip * v0.x + (barycentric.y / depth1) * wRecip * v1.x + (barycentric.z / depth2) * wRecip * v2.x,

(barycentric.x / depth0) * wRecip * v0.y + (barycentric.y / depth1) * wRecip * v1.y + (barycentric.z / depth2) * wRecip * v2.y

);

}
```

This function takes the barycentric coordinates, vertex positions, and depths of the triangle's vertices to perform perspective-correct interpolation of 2D values.

Shader interpolation techniques are vital for achieving smooth and realistic rendering in Vulkan applications. These techniques ensure that values are correctly interpolated across the surfaces of 3D objects, resulting in visually pleasing graphics. Depending on the specific rendering requirements, you can choose the appropriate interpolation method to achieve the desired visual effects.

Section 3.2: Stochastic Shading

STOCHASTIC SHADING is a rendering technique that introduces randomness into the shading process, creating more realistic and visually appealing results. Unlike traditional deterministic shading models, stochastic shading simulates the effects of randomness and variability in real-world materials and lighting. In this section, we will delve into the concept of stochastic shading, its applications, and how it can be implemented in Vulkan.

Understanding Stochastic Shading

STOCHASTIC SHADING acknowledges that many natural materials and lighting conditions exhibit random variations in their appearance. These variations are challenging to capture with deterministic shading models, which rely on fixed algorithms to simulate lighting and surface properties. Stochastic shading aims to introduce controlled randomness into the rendering pipeline to better mimic the complexities of the real world.

Applications of Stochastic Shading

STOCHASTIC SHADING finds applications in various areas of computer graphics:

1. Realistic Materials: Stochastic shading can be used to create more convincing materials like brushed metal, leather, and fabric, which exhibit subtle variations and imperfections in their appearance.

2. Natural Textures: It is well-suited for rendering natural textures such as wood, stone, and foliage, where irregular patterns and imperfections are common.

3. Procedural Generation: Stochastic shading is often used in procedural content generation to add randomness and variation to generated content, making it look less repetitive and more natural.

4. Environmental Effects: It can simulate environmental effects like raindrops on surfaces, dust particles in the air, and uneven terrain.

5. Artistic Style: Stochastic shading can also be used to achieve specific artistic styles, introducing controlled chaos and randomness to create unique visual effects.

Implementing Stochastic Shading in Vulkan

IMPLEMENTING STOCHASTIC shading in Vulkan requires introducing controlled randomness into the shading process. This can be achieved through various means, including the following techniques:

1. Noise Textures: *The most common approach is to use 2D or 3D noise textures. These textures contain precomputed random values that can be sampled in shaders to introduce randomness into lighting calculations or material properties.*

```
// SAMPLE A 2D NOISE texture

vec3 RandomOffset = texture(noiseTexture, uv).xyz;
```

2. Randomization Functions: *You can also use random number generators in shaders to produce random values for specific effects. These generators can be based on pseudo-random algorithms, ensuring reproducibility.*

```
// GENERATE A RANDOM number

float RandomValue = rand(seed);
```

3. Stochastic Sampling: *In some cases, stochastic shading involves sampling multiple times and averaging the results to simulate randomness. Techniques like Monte Carlo integration are commonly used for this purpose.*

4. Jittered Sampling: *Jittered sampling involves adding small random offsets to sample points in shaders, which can create a sense of randomness in shading calculations.*

```
// APPLY JITTERED SAMPLING

vec2 jitter = vec2(rand(seedX), rand(seedY));

vec2 sampledUV = uv + jitter;
```

5. Temporal Antialiasing: *In animation and real-time rendering,* *temporal antialiasing techniques can introduce randomness between frames to reduce aliasing artifacts.*

STOCHASTIC SHADING often requires careful tuning and balancing of randomness to achieve the desired visual effect without introducing excessive noise. Additionally, it may impact performance, so optimization is crucial, especially in real-time applications.

In summary, stochastic shading is a powerful technique for enhancing the realism and visual quality of Vulkan applications. By introducing controlled randomness into shaders, you can simulate the complexity and imperfections of real-world materials and lighting, resulting in more immersive and visually appealing graphics. The choice of stochastic shading method and the careful management of randomness depend on the specific rendering requirements and artistic goals of your application.

Section 3.3: Real-time Ray Tracing

REAL-TIME RAY TRACING is a cutting-edge rendering technique that simulates the behavior of light rays in a 3D scene to produce highly realistic and physically accurate images. It has gained prominence in recent years, driven by advancements in hardware and APIs like Vulkan that enable ray tracing in real-time applications. In this section, we will explore the concept of real-time ray tracing, its key components, and how it can be implemented using Vulkan.

Understanding Real-time Ray Tracing

REAL-TIME RAY TRACING is a rendering technique that traces rays of light as they interact with the objects and surfaces in a 3D scene. Unlike traditional rasterization, which projects 3D objects onto a 2D screen and simulates lighting effects through shaders, ray tracing calculates the path of individual rays of light, accounting for reflections, refractions, shadows, and global illumination.

Key Components of Real-time Ray Tracing:

1. **Ray Generation**: The rendering process begins with the generation of rays from the camera's viewpoint. Each pixel on the screen corresponds to a primary ray cast into the scene.

2. **Ray Intersection**: The rays are traced through the scene, and intersections with objects are computed. This involves testing whether a ray intersects with any object in the scene and determining the point of intersection.

3. **Shading and Lighting**: At each intersection point, shading calculations are performed. This includes evaluating material properties, applying lighting models, and considering the effects of shadows and reflections.

4. **Secondary Rays**: Ray tracing often involves the generation of secondary rays, such as reflection rays for reflective surfaces and refraction rays for transparent materials. These rays are traced recursively to simulate complex interactions.

5. **Global Illumination**: Real-time ray tracing can simulate global illumination, which considers indirect lighting effects, caustics, and the interreflection of light between surfaces.

Implementing Real-time Ray Tracing in Vulkan

IMPLEMENTING REAL-TIME ray tracing in Vulkan involves leveraging hardware-accelerated ray tracing capabilities and using the Vulkan ray tracing extension (VK_KHR_ray_tracing). Here are the fundamental steps to implement real-time ray tracing:

1. Ray Tracing Pipelines:

CREATE RAY TRACING pipelines that consist of shaders specifically designed for ray tracing. These shaders include ray generation shaders, intersection shaders, any-hit shaders, closest-hit shaders, and miss shaders, each responsible for different aspects of ray tracing.

// Example ray generation shader

#extension ... : raygen

layout(set = 0, binding = 0) **buffer** outputBuffer {

vec4 color;

};

void main() {

// Generate primary rays, trace them, and calculate final pixel color

color = TraceRays();

}

2. Bottom-level and Top-level Acceleration Structures:

CREATE ACCELERATION structures to efficiently traverse the scene geometry. Bottom-level acceleration structures represent individual objects or object instances, while top-level acceleration structures organize them into the scene hierarchy.

// Create and build acceleration structures

```
VkAccelerationStructureKHR          bottomLevelAS          =
CreateBottomLevelAS();

VkAccelerationStructureKHR          topLevelAS             =
CreateTopLevelAS(bottomLevelAS);
```

3. Ray Tracing Descriptors:

DEFINE DESCRIPTOR SETS and bindings for ray tracing shaders to access resources such as the acceleration structures, textures, and constant buffers.

```
// Create descriptor sets for ray tracing shaders

VkDescriptorSet descriptorSet = CreateRayTracingDescriptorSet();
```

4. Trace Rays:

IN THE RAY GENERATION shader, initiate ray tracing by tracing rays into the scene using Vulkan's ray tracing commands. This is where the primary rays are generated and traced through the scene.

```
// Trace rays in the ray generation shader

vkCmdTraceRaysKHR(commandBuffer,
raygenShaderBindingTable, ...);
```

5. Shader Binding Tables:

BUILD SHADER BINDING tables that associate shaders with ray tracing pipelines. These tables specify the entry points for each shader stage.

6. Render Loop:

IN THE APPLICATION'S render loop, dispatch ray tracing workloads and handle the results. This includes processing intersection, shading, and accumulation of pixel colors.

Real-time ray tracing in Vulkan introduces remarkable visual quality improvements but also demands significant computational resources. It is particularly suitable for applications that require photorealistic rendering, such as gaming, architectural visualization, and film production. As hardware support for ray tracing continues to evolve, Vulkan remains a powerful platform for implementing this advanced rendering technique.

Section 3.4: Subsurface Scattering Implementation

SUBSURFACE SCATTERING (SSS) is a rendering technique used to simulate the behavior of light as it penetrates and scatters within translucent materials like skin, wax, and marble. It plays a critical role in achieving realistic and convincing visual effects in computer graphics. In this section, we will explore the concept of subsurface scattering, its significance in rendering, and how it can be implemented using Vulkan.

Understanding Subsurface Scattering

SUBSURFACE SCATTERING refers to the phenomenon where light enters the surface of a translucent object, scatters within the material, and then exits at a different point. This scattering effect occurs due to the interaction between light and the material's internal structure, such as the distribution of pores, fibers, or cells.

Importance of Subsurface Scattering:

- **Realism**: SSS adds realism to rendered objects by simulating the soft, diffuse appearance of translucent materials.

- **Visual Depth**: It provides depth and volume to objects, making them appear more lifelike and less flat.

- **Skin Rendering**: SSS is particularly important for rendering human skin, as it mimics the way light interacts with multiple layers of tissue beneath the skin's surface.

- **Materials**: It is used for rendering materials like wax, milk, leaves, and certain types of plastics.

Implementing Subsurface Scattering in Vulkan

IMPLEMENTING SUBSURFACE scattering in Vulkan involves complex calculations to simulate the scattering of light within translucent materials. Here are the fundamental steps to implement SSS:

1. Light Transport Simulation:

SIMULATE THE TRANSPORT of light within the material using techniques like diffusion theory. This involves modeling how photons scatter and diffuse within the material, creating a volumetric representation of the light distribution.

2. Material Properties:

DEFINE MATERIAL PROPERTIES that influence SSS, such as the scattering coefficient, absorption coefficient, and the phase function. These properties determine how light scatters and attenuates within the material.

3. Multiple Scattering:

CONSIDER MULTIPLE SCATTERING events, where light can enter and exit the material at different locations. Multiple scattering contributes to the soft, diffuse appearance of SSS.

4. Sampling and Integration:

USE SAMPLING AND INTEGRATION techniques to calculate the contribution of SSS at each point on the material's surface. This involves tracing rays and accumulating the scattered light from multiple directions.

```glsl
// Example shader code for SSS integration

vec3 ComputeSubsurfaceScattering(in vec3 surfacePos, in vec3 viewDir) {

vec3 scatteredLight = vec3(0.0);

// Perform sampling and integration here

return scatteredLight;

}
```

5. Shading and Rendering:

INCORPORATE THE COMPUTED SSS contribution into the shading model of the material. This can include adding it to the diffuse component of the material's appearance.

6. Performance Considerations:

SSS CALCULATIONS CAN be computationally expensive. Consider optimization techniques such as precomputation, caching, and hardware acceleration to achieve real-time performance.

7. Artistic Control:

PROVIDE CONTROLS FOR artists and developers to adjust the appearance of SSS, including the scattering coefficients and the scale of the effect.

8. Scene Lighting:

ENSURE THAT THE LIGHTING in the scene is suitable for SSS. Realistic lighting, including directional, point, and environment lighting, contributes to the visual fidelity of SSS.

Implementing subsurface scattering in Vulkan requires a deep understanding of the underlying physics and mathematics involved in light transport within translucent materials. It is a technique often used in conjunction with other rendering effects to create convincing and visually appealing scenes. When correctly implemented, SSS enhances the realism of rendered materials and is particularly valuable for character rendering and scenes with organic or translucent objects.

Section 3.5: Real-time Global Illumination Techniques

REAL-TIME GLOBAL ILLUMINATION (RTGI) is a rendering technique used to simulate indirect lighting effects in a scene, providing realistic and dynamic lighting interactions. Global illumination includes phenomena like diffuse interreflection, color bleeding, and soft shadows that occur when light bounces off surfaces and affects the appearance of other objects. In this section, we will explore the concept of real-time global illumination, its significance in rendering, and how it can be implemented using Vulkan.

Understanding Real-time Global Illumination

GLOBAL ILLUMINATION is a fundamental component of achieving photorealism in computer graphics. It accounts for the indirect lighting in a scene, where light from a source not only directly illuminates surfaces but also bounces off and indirectly affects the illumination of nearby objects. RTGI aims to simulate these complex lighting interactions in real time, providing visually stunning and immersive rendering results.

Significance of Real-time Global Illumination:

- **Realism**: RTGI enhances the realism of scenes by simulating how light interacts with surfaces, creating soft and natural-looking shadows, and introducing color bleeding effects.

- **Dynamic Environments**: It is essential for rendering dynamic environments where lighting conditions change over time, such as day-night cycles or moving light sources.

- **Complex Materials**: RTGI is particularly valuable for rendering scenes with materials that exhibit subsurface scattering, translucency, or intricate surface properties.

Implementing Real-time Global Illumination in Vulkan

IMPLEMENTING RTGI IN Vulkan is a complex and computationally intensive task. It requires advanced techniques to simulate the behavior of light as it bounces around the scene. Here are the fundamental steps to implement RTGI:

1. Ray Tracing or Radiosity:

CHOOSE BETWEEN RAY tracing-based or radiosity-based approaches to simulate global illumination. Ray tracing involves tracing rays of light as they bounce and interact with surfaces, while radiosity focuses on energy transfer between surfaces.

2. Scene Representation:

CREATE AN APPROPRIATE representation of the scene that includes information about geometry, materials, and light sources. This representation is used to compute the indirect lighting.

3. Ray Tracing Pass:

IN A RAY TRACING-BASED approach, perform a ray tracing pass to compute the paths of light rays as they interact with surfaces. Trace rays for reflections, refractions, and global illumination effects.

```
// Example shader code for ray tracing

vec3 TraceRay(vec3 rayOrigin, vec3 rayDirection) {

vec3 color = vec3(0.0);

// Perform ray tracing calculations here

return color;

}
```

4. Radiosity Computation:

IN A RADIOSITY-BASED approach, compute the radiosity of surfaces by solving a system of linear equations that describe the transfer of energy between surfaces.

5. Shading Integration:

INTEGRATE THE COMPUTED global illumination into the shading model of materials. This includes adjusting the diffuse and specular components to account for indirect lighting.

6. Multiple Bounces:

CONSIDER MULTIPLE BOUNCES of light rays to simulate complex indirect lighting interactions. This involves tracing rays recursively as they bounce off surfaces.

7. Performance Optimization:

RTGI IS COMPUTATIONALLY expensive. Employ performance optimization techniques, such as parallel processing, level of detail, and hierarchical acceleration structures, to achieve real-time frame rates.

8. *Artistic Control:*

PROVIDE CONTROLS FOR artists and developers to adjust the intensity, color, and other properties of global illumination to achieve the desired visual effect.

Real-time global illumination is a challenging rendering technique that significantly contributes to the realism and visual quality of rendered scenes. When implemented effectively, it enhances the overall lighting, shading, and atmosphere of a 3D environment, making it a valuable tool for various applications, including gaming, architectural visualization, and film production. Vulkan's capabilities in ray tracing and advanced rendering make it a suitable platform for implementing RTGI in real-time applications.

Chapter 4: Deep Learning in Graphics

Section 4.1: Neural Networks for Procedural Content

Neural networks have revolutionized many fields, including computer graphics. In the context of graphics, they offer a powerful tool for generating procedural content, which includes textures, models, animations, and even entire game levels. In this section, we will explore how neural networks can be applied to procedural content generation, their advantages, and some practical examples.

Procedural Content Generation (PCG)

PROCEDURAL CONTENT generation is the technique of generating game content algorithmically rather than creating it manually. It has been a crucial component in game development, as it allows for the creation of vast and diverse game worlds with reduced development time and storage requirements. PCG can be used to create terrain, textures, levels, characters, and more.

Neural Networks in PCG

1. Texture Synthesis:

NEURAL NETWORKS CAN be trained to generate high-quality textures that exhibit a wide range of patterns and details. By training on a dataset of textures, a neural network can learn to create new textures that are visually similar to those in the training set.

```python
# Example code for texture synthesis using a neural network

import tensorflow as tf

# Load a pre-trained neural network for texture synthesis

model = tf.keras.applications.VGG19(include_top=False, weights='imagenet')

# Generate a new texture

new_texture = generate_texture(model, seed=123)
```

2. Terrain Generation:

GENERATING REALISTIC terrain for games or simulations is a complex task. Neural networks can be used to create heightmaps that represent terrain features like mountains, valleys, and rivers. These heightmaps can then be used to create 3D terrain meshes.

```python
# Example code for terrain generation using a neural network

import tensorflow as tf

# Define a neural network model for terrain generation

model = tf.keras.Sequential([

tf.keras.layers.Dense(256, activation='relu', input_dim=100),

tf.keras.layers.Dense(512, activation='relu'),

tf.keras.layers.Dense(1024, activation='relu'),

tf.keras.layers.Dense(4096, activation='relu'),

tf.keras.layers.Reshape((64, 64, 1))
```

```
])
```

```
# Generate a terrain heightmap
```

```
heightmap = generate_terrain(model, noise_seed=123)
```

3. Level Design:

NEURAL NETWORKS CAN assist in generating game levels that are both challenging and engaging. They can learn from existing levels and create new ones that are balanced and enjoyable for players.

```
# Example code for level design using a neural network
```

```
import tensorflow as tf
```

```
# Define a neural network model for level generation
```

```
model = tf.keras.Sequential([
```

```
tf.keras.layers.LSTM(128, return_sequences=True, input_shape=(10, 64)),
```

```
tf.keras.layers.LSTM(128, return_sequences=True),
```

```
tf.keras.layers.Dense(64, activation='softmax')
```

```
])
```

```
# Generate a game level layout
```

```
level_layout = generate_level(model, seed=456)
```

Advantages of Neural Networks in PCG

1. **Flexibility**: Neural networks can learn complex patterns

and relationships from data, allowing for the generation of diverse and realistic content.

2. **Speed**: Once trained, neural networks can generate content quickly, reducing the time required for content creation.

3. **Variability**: Neural networks can introduce variability in generated content, making it less repetitive and more interesting for players.

4. **Scalability**: They can be scaled to generate content at different levels of detail, from small textures to entire game worlds.

5. **Adaptability**: Neural networks can adapt to different art styles and genres, making them versatile for various game development needs.

Challenges and Considerations

WHILE NEURAL NETWORKS offer great potential for procedural content generation, there are challenges and considerations:

1. **Training Data**: Neural networks require large and diverse training datasets to generate high-quality content.

2. **Overfitting**: Ensuring that generated content is not too similar to the training data (overfitting) can be a challenge.

3. **Model Complexity**: Designing and training effective neural network architectures for PCG can be complex.

4. **Interactivity**: Integrating neural network-based PCG into real-time game engines and ensuring player interactivity can be challenging.

In summary, neural networks have opened up exciting possibilities for procedural content generation in computer graphics. They enable the creation of content that is both visually appealing and diverse, enhancing the overall gaming and graphics experience. However, successful implementation requires careful consideration of data, model design, and integration into the development pipeline.

Section 4.2: Style Transfer in Real-time Rendering

STYLE TRANSFER IS A fascinating technique in deep learning and computer graphics that allows you to apply the artistic style of one image or artwork to another. It has gained popularity for its ability to create visually stunning and unique renderings. In this section, we will delve into style transfer in the context of real-time rendering, its applications, and how it can be implemented using Vulkan.

Understanding Style Transfer

STYLE TRANSFER IS BASED on the idea that the artistic style of an image can be separated from its content. Given two images, one serving as the content source and the other as the style source, the goal is to generate a new image that combines the content of the former with the artistic style of the latter.

Key Components of Style Transfer:

1. **Content Image**: The content image represents the subject or objects you want to render in a particular style.
2. **Style Image**: The style image defines the artistic characteristics you want to apply to the content.
3. **Generated Image**: The generated image is the result of the style transfer process, combining the content and style.
4. **Loss Functions**: Style transfer uses loss functions to

measure the difference between the content and style of the generated image and the original images.

Applications of Style Transfer in Real-time Rendering

STYLE TRANSFER HAS various applications in real-time rendering:

1. Artistic Rendering: It allows artists and designers to create unique and visually appealing renderings by applying various artistic styles to their scenes.

2. Game Development: Game developers can use style transfer to dynamically change the visual style of a game world based on player actions or game events.

3. Content Generation: Style transfer can be applied to procedural content generation, allowing for the creation of game assets with specific styles.

4. Non-Photorealistic Rendering (NPR): NPR techniques, such as cartoon rendering or painting-like effects, can benefit from style transfer to achieve distinct visual styles.

5. Augmented Reality (AR): In AR applications, style transfer can be used to seamlessly blend virtual objects with the real world by matching their visual styles.

Implementing Style Transfer in Vulkan

IMPLEMENTING REAL-TIME style transfer in Vulkan involves several steps:

1. Pre-trained Models:

USE PRE-TRAINED DEEP learning models, such as convolutional neural networks (CNNs), that are capable of performing style transfer. Models like VGG and ResNet are commonly used for this purpose.

 # Example code for loading a pre-trained VGG model for style transfer

import torch

import torchvision.models **as** models

 # Load a pre-trained VGG model

vgg_model = models.vgg19(pretrained=True)

2. Content and Style Layers:

IDENTIFY SPECIFIC LAYERS in the model that capture content and style information. Content layers represent the features of the content image, while style layers represent the features of the style image.

 # Define content and style layers for VGG

content_layers = ['conv_4']

style_layers = ['conv_1', 'conv_2', 'conv_3', 'conv_4', 'conv_5']

3. Loss Functions:

DEFINE LOSS FUNCTIONS that measure the difference between the features of the generated image and the content and style images. These loss functions guide the optimization process.

```
# Example code for defining content and style loss functions

content_loss = ContentLoss(content_layers)

style_loss = StyleLoss(style_layers)
```

4. Optimization:

USE AN OPTIMIZATION algorithm, such as gradient descent, to minimize the total loss, which is a combination of the content and style losses.

```
# Example code for optimizing the generated image

optimizer = torch.optim.LBFGS([generated_image])

for i in range(num_steps):

def closure():

optimizer.zero_grad()

content_out, style_out = model(generated_image)

content_loss(content_out, content_target)

style_loss(style_out, style_target)

total_loss = content_loss.loss + style_loss.loss

total_loss.backward()

return total_loss

optimizer.step(closure)
```

5. Real-time Updates:

TO ACHIEVE REAL-TIME style transfer, optimize the generated image iteratively and update it in the rendering pipeline.

6. User Interaction:

PROVIDE USER CONTROLS to adjust the intensity and parameters of style transfer to achieve the desired visual effect.

Real-time style transfer can significantly enhance the visual appeal of computer graphics applications by enabling the creation of unique and artistic renderings. While it can be computationally intensive, especially with high-resolution images, it offers exciting opportunities for creative expression in real-time rendering using Vulkan.

Section 4.3: AI-driven Animation

AI-DRIVEN ANIMATION is a cutting-edge application of artificial intelligence and machine learning in computer graphics. It involves using AI algorithms to automate and enhance the animation process, making it more efficient and capable of producing lifelike and dynamic animations. In this section, we will explore AI-driven animation techniques, their significance in the industry, and how they can be integrated into real-time rendering using Vulkan.

Understanding AI-driven Animation

AI-DRIVEN ANIMATION leverages machine learning techniques to automate various aspects of the animation pipeline. This includes tasks such as character animation, motion capture, facial animation, and even procedural animation generation. AI can analyze and learn from existing animations and then generate new animations that follow the same style and motion principles.

Key Components of AI-driven Animation:

1. **Data Collection**: AI-driven animation often starts with the collection of animation data, including motion capture data, keyframe animations, and reference animations.
2. **Machine Learning Models**: Machine learning models, such as neural networks, are trained on this data to learn the underlying patterns and styles of animation.
3. **Motion Synthesis**: AI algorithms can synthesize new animations by combining learned motion patterns and generating smooth transitions between different actions.
4. **Real-time Control**: AI-driven animation can be integrated into real-time applications, allowing for dynamic and responsive character animations in games and simulations.

Significance of AI-driven Animation

AI-DRIVEN ANIMATION offers several advantages in the field of computer graphics:

1. Realism: It enables the creation of realistic and natural animations that mimic the nuances of human or creature movements, enhancing the overall immersion in virtual worlds.

2. Efficiency: AI-driven animation can significantly reduce the time and effort required for animators to create complex animations manually.

3. Variation: It allows for the generation of a wide variety of animations, making characters and objects in games and simulations appear more dynamic and lifelike.

4. Consistency: AI-driven animations maintain a consistent style and quality, ensuring that characters and objects behave predictably.

5. Interactivity: Integration with real-time rendering and physics engines enables dynamic and interactive animations that respond to user input.

Implementing AI-driven Animation in Vulkan

INTEGRATING AI-DRIVEN animation into Vulkan-based applications involves several steps:

1. Data Collection:

COLLECT ANIMATION DATA, which may include motion capture data, keyframe animations, or reference animations that serve as training data for AI models.

2. Model Selection:

CHOOSE OR DESIGN AN appropriate machine learning model for animation synthesis. Recurrent neural networks (RNNs), convolutional neural networks (CNNs), and generative adversarial networks (GANs) are commonly used for this purpose.

```python
# Example code for defining a simple RNN model for animation synthesis
import tensorflow as tf
```

```
model = tf.keras.Sequential([

tf.keras.layers.LSTM(128,                    return_sequences=True,
input_shape=(sequence_length, feature_dim)),

tf.keras.layers.LSTM(128, return_sequences=True),

tf.keras.layers.Dense(output_dim)

])
```

3. Training:

TRAIN THE AI MODEL on the collected animation data to learn the patterns and styles of animation. Training may involve optimizing model parameters to minimize the difference between synthesized animations and the training data.

4. Real-time Integration:

INTEGRATE THE TRAINED AI model into the Vulkan-based rendering pipeline. This may involve passing input data such as user controls or physics simulations to the AI model and receiving animated character or object poses in real time.

```
# Example code for real-time animation control

while running:

user_input = get_user_input()

physics_simulation = simulate_physics()

ai_output = ai_model(user_input, physics_simulation)

update_character_pose(ai_output)
```

render_frame()

5. User Interaction:

PROVIDE USER CONTROLS or game logic that allows users to interact with and influence AI-driven animations. This could include real-time character control, animation blending, or response to in-game events.

AI-driven animation in Vulkan-based applications opens up possibilities for creating dynamic and responsive animations that enhance the overall user experience. Whether it's character animations in games or simulations, procedural animations for objects, or interactive storytelling, AI-driven animation is becoming an indispensable tool for graphics developers looking to achieve realistic and captivating animations.

Section 4.4: Neural Networks in Texture Generation

TEXTURE GENERATION plays a crucial role in computer graphics, as it determines the appearance of surfaces and objects in 3D environments. Neural networks have emerged as powerful tools for creating high-quality textures, enhancing the realism of rendered scenes. In this section, we will explore the application of neural networks in texture generation, their advantages, and how they can be integrated into real-time rendering using Vulkan.

Understanding Neural Networks in Texture Generation

TEXTURE GENERATION using neural networks involves training models to generate textures that exhibit various patterns, details, and styles. Neural networks can learn the statistical properties of textures from training data and then generate new textures that are visually similar to those in the training set.

Key Components of Texture Generation with Neural Networks:

1. **Training Data**: A dataset of textures is collected to train the neural network. This dataset includes a variety of textures with different styles, colors, and patterns.
2. **Neural Network Model**: The neural network architecture is designed to take random input noise and generate textures. Variations of generative models like Generative Adversarial Networks (GANs) and Variational Autoencoders (VAEs) are commonly used.
3. **Loss Functions**: Loss functions are defined to measure the difference between the generated textures and the real textures in the training set. These loss functions guide the training process.

Advantages of Neural Networks in Texture Generation

TEXTURE GENERATION with neural networks offers several advantages in computer graphics:

1. **Realism**: Neural networks can produce highly realistic textures with intricate details and patterns, enhancing the visual fidelity of 3D scenes.
2. **Variability**: They enable the creation of diverse textures, reducing the repetition of patterns and making scenes appear more natural.
3. **Efficiency**: Texture generation with neural networks can save time and effort compared to manual texture creation.

4. **Seamlessness**: Generated textures can seamlessly tile and blend with one another, avoiding visible seams in the rendered scene.
5. **Style Transfer**: Neural networks can apply artistic styles or transfer textures from one source to another, allowing for creative customization.

Implementing Neural Networks in Texture Generation with Vulkan

INTEGRATING NEURAL networks into Vulkan-based applications for texture generation involves the following steps:

1. **Data Collection and Preprocessing**:

– Collect a dataset of textures representing the desired style or patterns.

– Preprocess the textures to ensure consistency in size, format, and color space.

1. **Neural Network Model**:

– Choose or design a neural network model suitable for texture generation. GANs and VAEs are popular choices.

– Train the model on the prepared dataset to learn the statistical properties of textures.

1. **Texture Synthesis**:

– Use the trained neural network to synthesize new textures by feeding it random noise as input.

– Generate textures with the desired style or characteristics.

1. **Texture Tiling**:

– Ensure that generated textures can tile seamlessly when applied to surfaces in the 3D environment.

1. **Real-time Integration**:

– Integrate the neural network-based texture generation into the Vulkan rendering pipeline.

– Apply generated textures to objects or surfaces in the scene during rendering.

```
// Example Vulkan code for applying generated textures

void    RenderObjectWithGeneratedTexture(VkCommandBuffer commandBuffer, VkImage generatedTexture) {

// Bind the generated texture as a texture sampler

vkCmdBindImage(commandBuffer,
VK_DESCRIPTOR_SET_TEXTURE, generatedTexture);

// Render the object using the generated texture

// ...

}
```

1. **User Interaction**:

– Provide controls or parameters that allow users to customize generated textures or apply different styles in real time.

Neural networks in texture generation offer an exciting avenue for enhancing the visual quality and realism of computer graphics applications. Whether it's creating realistic materials for game environments, generating artistic textures for scenes, or enabling user customization, the integration of neural networks in Vulkan-based rendering pipelines can significantly contribute to the overall visual appeal and immersion of 3D worlds.

Section 4.5: Advanced AI for Game Logic

ADVANCED ARTIFICIAL intelligence (AI) techniques have become pivotal in modern game development, enabling more immersive and dynamic gameplay experiences. In this section, we will explore the application of advanced AI for game logic, its significance in gaming, and how it can be seamlessly integrated into real-time rendering using Vulkan.

Understanding Advanced AI for Game Logic

ADVANCED AI FOR GAME logic encompasses a wide range of techniques and algorithms that enable non-player characters (NPCs) and entities within a game to exhibit intelligent behavior, react to player actions, make decisions, and contribute to the overall gameplay experience. These AI systems can range from pathfinding and decision-making to procedural content generation and adaptive difficulty adjustment.

Key Components of Advanced AI for Game Logic:

1. **Decision-Making Algorithms**: Advanced AI often involves complex decision-making processes that consider multiple factors, goals, and constraints. Techniques like behavior trees, utility-based AI, and reinforcement learning are used.
2. **Pathfinding and Navigation**: Pathfinding algorithms, such as A* and Dijkstra's, are employed to enable NPCs to navigate through game environments efficiently.
3. **Procedural Content Generation**: AI-driven procedural content generation techniques can create dynamic and unpredictable game worlds, levels, and challenges.
4. **Adaptive Difficulty**: AI can adjust game difficulty in real time based on player performance, ensuring an engaging and balanced experience.
5. **Natural Language Processing (NLP)**: NLP AI can enable NPCs to understand and respond to player text or voice inputs, enhancing the interactivity of the game.

Significance of Advanced AI in Gaming

ADVANCED AI FOR GAME logic plays a critical role in shaping the gaming experience:

1. **Immersive Gameplay**: It enhances player immersion by providing challenging opponents, realistic NPC behavior, and dynamic environments.
2. **Dynamic Content**: AI-driven procedural content generation ensures that no two playthroughs are the same, increasing replayability.
3. **Player Interaction**: AI can create opportunities for meaningful player-NPC interactions, dialogues, and

decision-making that affect the game's narrative.

4. **Balanced Difficulty**: Adaptive AI helps maintain an appropriate level of challenge for players, keeping the game engaging without being frustratingly difficult.

5. **Emergent Gameplay**: Advanced AI can lead to emergent gameplay experiences, where unexpected and complex interactions between game elements occur.

Implementing Advanced AI in Vulkan-Based Games

INTEGRATING ADVANCED AI into Vulkan-based games involves several key steps:

1. **AI Model Selection**: Choose or design AI models that are appropriate for the specific AI tasks in the game. For example, use behavior trees for NPC decision-making or machine learning models for adaptive difficulty.

2. **Data Collection and Training**: Collect and preprocess data as needed for training AI models. Train the models on relevant datasets or in-game data.

3. **Real-time Integration**: Integrate the trained AI models into the game engine and rendering pipeline to enable real-time decision-making and behavior.

```
// Example Vulkan code for integrating AI into game logic

void UpdateNPCBehavior(VkCommandBuffer commandBuffer, AIModel npcAI) {

// Update the NPC's behavior using the AI model

// ...

}
```

1. **User Interaction**: Implement user interfaces or systems that allow players to interact with AI-controlled entities, such as initiating conversations with NPCs or influencing their decisions.
2. **Content Generation**: Utilize AI-driven procedural content generation to create dynamic game worlds, levels, quests, or challenges.
3. **Feedback and Testing**: Continuously test and refine the AI systems based on player feedback to ensure that the AI enhances rather than detracts from the gaming experience.

Advanced AI for game logic powered by Vulkan can elevate games to new levels of complexity and immersion. Whether it's creating lifelike NPC behavior, generating procedurally generated content, or adapting gameplay to individual player preferences, advanced AI techniques are a driving force behind the evolution of modern gaming. As hardware and software technologies continue to advance, AI-powered game logic is likely to play an even more prominent role in the future of interactive entertainment.

Chapter 5: Advanced Simulation Techniques

Section 5.1: Fluid and Gas Dynamics

Fluid and gas dynamics simulation is a crucial component of many computer graphics applications, including games, movies, and engineering simulations. It involves modeling the behavior of liquids and gases in a virtual environment, allowing for realistic visual effects and dynamic interactions. In this section, we will delve into fluid and gas dynamics simulation, its applications, numerical methods, and how it can be implemented in real-time rendering using Vulkan.

Understanding Fluid and Gas Dynamics Simulation

FLUID AND GAS DYNAMICS simulation aims to replicate the behavior of fluids (liquids and gases) in a computer-generated environment. These simulations are based on the fundamental principles of fluid dynamics, including the Navier-Stokes equations, which describe the motion of fluids. The simulation calculates properties like velocity, pressure, and density of the fluid at each point in space and time.

Key Components of Fluid and Gas Dynamics Simulation:

1. **Navier-Stokes Equations**: These partial differential equations govern fluid motion and are solved numerically to simulate fluid behavior.
2. **Grid-based Representation**: Simulations often use a grid-

based representation of the fluid domain, with each cell storing fluid properties.

3. **Boundary Conditions**: Defining boundary conditions is essential to simulate interactions between the fluid and objects in the environment.

4. **Time Integration**: Simulations are updated over time steps using numerical integration methods, such as the Euler method or more advanced techniques like the Runge-Kutta method.

Applications of Fluid and Gas Dynamics Simulation

FLUID AND GAS DYNAMICS simulation finds applications in various fields:

1. **Visual Effects**: In movies and video games, it creates realistic fluid animations, including water, smoke, fire, and explosions.

2. **Engineering**: Simulations help engineers study fluid flow in real-world scenarios, such as aerodynamics, HVAC systems, and fluid transport.

3. **Weather Simulation**: Weather prediction models rely on fluid dynamics simulations to forecast atmospheric conditions.

4. **Medical Visualization**: Simulations assist in visualizing blood flow and simulating the behavior of fluids in the human body.

5. **Game Physics**: Games use fluid simulations for effects like water ripples, splashes, and particle-based fluids.

Numerical Methods for Fluid Simulation

FLUID SIMULATIONS REQUIRE solving complex differential equations numerically. Common numerical methods include:

1. **Finite Difference Methods**: These discretize the Navier-Stokes equations on a grid, approximating derivatives using finite differences.
2. **SPH (Smoothed Particle Hydrodynamics)**: SPH is a particle-based method where fluid properties are associated with particles. It's suitable for simulating free-surface flows and interacting fluids.
3. **Lattice Boltzmann Method**: LBM is a mesoscopic method that simulates fluid flow based on the movement of particles between grid cells.
4. **Finite Element Method (FEM)**: FEM is used for solving specialized fluid problems, such as simulating fluid-structure interactions.

Implementing Fluid Simulation in Vulkan

INTEGRATING FLUID AND gas dynamics simulation into Vulkan-based applications involves several steps:

1. **Grid Setup**: Create a grid-based representation of the fluid domain within Vulkan.
2. **Numerical Solver**: Implement a numerical solver to advance the simulation over time steps, solving the Navier-Stokes equations.
3. **Boundary Handling**: Define boundary conditions to handle interactions with objects or surfaces in the environment.
4. **Rendering**: Visualize the fluid simulation by rendering the properties of the fluid (e.g., density, velocity) using Vulkan

shaders.

5. **Real-time Interaction**: Provide mechanisms for real-time interaction, such as adding forces or obstacles to the fluid.

6. **Performance Optimization**: Optimize the simulation for real-time rendering by utilizing Vulkan's parallel processing capabilities and GPU acceleration.

```
// Example Vulkan code for rendering fluid simulation

void RenderFluidSimulation(VkCommandBuffer commandBuffer,
FluidSimulation fluidSim) {

// Bind fluid simulation data buffers

vkCmdBindBuffer(commandBuffer,
VK_DESCRIPTOR_SET_FLUID_DATA,
fluidSim.getDataBuffer());

// Render the fluid using Vulkan shaders

// ...

}
```

Fluid and gas dynamics simulation in Vulkan opens up possibilities for creating realistic and visually captivating animations and effects in real-time applications. Whether it's simulating water for games, studying airflow in engineering, or generating impressive visual effects, fluid simulation is a powerful tool in the arsenal of computer graphics developers, made even more accessible with the capabilities of Vulkan.

Section 5.2: Rigid Body Dynamics

RIGID BODY DYNAMICS is a fundamental component of physics simulation in computer graphics. It deals with the motion and interactions of solid objects that maintain their shape and do not deform under external forces. In this section, we will explore rigid body dynamics, its applications, numerical methods for simulation, and how it can be implemented in real-time rendering using Vulkan.

Understanding Rigid Body Dynamics

RIGID BODIES ARE OBJECTS whose shape and size remain constant as they move through space. Rigid body dynamics simulates the motion of these objects, including their translation and rotation, and their interactions with other rigid bodies and the environment. This simulation relies on Newtonian physics principles, including equations of motion, forces, and torques.

Key Components of Rigid Body Dynamics:

1. **Rigid Body Representation**: Objects are represented as rigid bodies with properties like mass, inertia, and shape.
2. **Forces and Torques**: External forces, such as gravity, friction, and user-defined forces, act on rigid bodies, causing translational and rotational motion.
3. **Collision Detection**: Detecting collisions between rigid bodies and the environment or other objects is essential for resolving interactions.
4. **Contact Resolution**: When collisions occur, contact resolution algorithms determine how objects respond, including bouncing, sliding, or sticking.

Applications of Rigid Body Dynamics

RIGID BODY DYNAMICS simulation has diverse applications in computer graphics and beyond:

1. **Game Physics**: In video games, it enables realistic object interactions, including character movement, object stacking, and vehicle dynamics.
2. **Virtual Prototyping**: Engineers use it for simulating mechanical systems and testing designs before physical construction.
3. **Animation**: It aids in creating realistic animations of objects and characters in movies and simulations.
4. **Robotics**: Rigid body dynamics is essential for simulating the motion and interactions of robots and robotic components.
5. **Medical Simulation**: In medical applications, it helps simulate the behavior of anatomical structures and medical devices.

Numerical Methods for Rigid Body Dynamics

SIMULATING RIGID BODY dynamics involves solving differential equations numerically. Common numerical methods include:

1. **Euler's Method**: A simple method that updates object positions and rotations based on forces and torques at each time step.
2. **Verlet Integration**: A more stable method that uses position and velocity updates to compute new positions.
3. **Runge-Kutta Methods**: Higher-order methods that provide accurate integration but are computationally more expensive.

4. **Impulse-Based Methods**: These methods resolve collisions by calculating and applying impulses to objects to correct their positions and velocities.

Implementing Rigid Body Dynamics in Vulkan

INTEGRATING RIGID BODY dynamics into Vulkan-based applications involves several steps:

1. **Rigid Body Representation**: Define a representation for rigid bodies, including their mass, inertia, shape, and initial positions and orientations.
2. **Force and Torque Calculation**: Implement the calculation of forces and torques acting on rigid bodies, including gravity, user inputs, and other external forces.
3. **Numerical Integration**: Choose a numerical integration method to update rigid body positions and rotations at each time step.

```
// Example Vulkan code for updating rigid body positions using Euler's method

void UpdateRigidBodyPosition(VkCommandBuffer commandBuffer, RigidBody body, float deltaTime) {

// Calculate forces and torques acting on the body

CalculateForcesAndTorques(body);

// Update position and orientation using Euler's method

body.position += body.velocity * deltaTime;

body.orientation += body.angularVelocity * deltaTime;

}
```

1. **Collision Detection and Resolution**: Implement collision detection algorithms to identify collisions between rigid bodies and resolve them using appropriate contact resolution methods.

2. **Rendering Integration**: Render the rigid bodies using Vulkan's rendering capabilities to visualize their motion and interactions in the scene.

3. **Real-time Interaction**: Allow user interactions or scripted events to affect rigid bodies in real time, such as applying forces, constraints, or triggers.

Rigid body dynamics simulation in Vulkan empowers developers to create realistic object interactions and animations, whether it's for game physics, engineering simulations, or other interactive applications. By integrating physics-based simulations into the rendering pipeline, Vulkan-based applications can achieve a high level of realism and interactivity, enhancing the overall user experience.

Section 5.3: Soft Body Simulation with Finite Elements

SOFT BODY SIMULATION is a specialized area of physics simulation in computer graphics that deals with deformable objects. Unlike rigid bodies, soft bodies can change shape and deform under external forces, making them suitable for simulating objects like cloth, rubber, and soft tissues. In this section, we will explore soft body simulation with finite elements, its applications, numerical methods, and how it can be implemented in real-time rendering using Vulkan.

Understanding Soft Body Simulation with Finite Elements

SOFT BODY SIMULATION with finite elements is based on the principles of continuum mechanics and numerical methods. It divides a deformable object into smaller elements and models their behavior using equations that describe stress, strain, and deformation. These equations are solved numerically to simulate the dynamic behavior of soft bodies under various forces.

Key Components of Soft Body Simulation:

1. **Mesh Representation**: Soft bodies are typically represented as meshes composed of elements (tetrahedra, triangles, etc.) that can deform independently.
2. **Material Properties**: Each element is assigned material properties, such as stiffness, damping, and density, which dictate how it responds to deformation and forces.
3. **Equations of Motion**: Continuum mechanics equations, such as the linear elasticity equations or the Neo-Hookean model, describe the relationship between stress and strain in the material.
4. **Numerical Solvers**: Numerical methods, like the Finite Element Method (FEM) or the Mass-Spring System, are used to solve the equations of motion for the soft body.

Applications of Soft Body Simulation

SOFT BODY SIMULATION is used in various applications across computer graphics and engineering:

1. **Cloth Simulation**: It's essential for creating realistic clothing and fabric motion in games, movies, and virtual

fashion design.

2. **Character Animation**: Soft body simulation can be applied to simulate the skin and muscles of characters, making their movements more natural.

3. **Medical Simulation**: In medical applications, it helps simulate soft tissues and organs for surgical training and visualization.

4. **Engineering Analysis**: Engineers use it to study the behavior of deformable materials in structural analysis and product design.

Numerical Methods for Soft Body Simulation

SIMULATING SOFT BODIES involves solving complex equations of motion numerically. Two common numerical methods are:

1. **Finite Element Method (FEM)**: FEM discretizes the soft body into finite elements, allowing for accurate modeling of complex materials and shapes. It's widely used in engineering and computer graphics.

2. **Mass-Spring System**: This method models the soft body as a collection of mass points connected by springs. While less accurate than FEM, it's computationally efficient and suitable for real-time simulations.

Implementing Soft Body Simulation in Vulkan

INTEGRATING SOFT BODY simulation with finite elements into Vulkan-based applications involves several steps:

1. **Mesh Representation**: Create a mesh representation of the soft body using appropriate data structures, including vertices, elements, and material properties.

2. **Numerical Solver**: Implement a numerical solver that can solve the equations of motion for the soft body's elements. This may involve using FEM or a mass-spring system.

3. **Time Integration**: Update the soft body's positions and deformations over time steps using numerical integration methods, such as the implicit Euler method.

// Example Vulkan code for updating soft body deformations using implicit Euler method

```
void                UpdateSoftBodyDeformation(VkCommandBuffer commandBuffer, SoftBody softBody, float deltaTime) {

// Calculate internal forces and deformations

CalculateInternalForcesAndDeformations(softBody);

// Update soft body deformations using implicit Euler method

UpdateDeformationsImplicitly(softBody, deltaTime);

}
```

1. **Collision Detection**: Implement collision detection algorithms to detect and respond to collisions between the soft body and other objects or the environment.

2. **Rendering Integration**: Render the soft body using Vulkan's rendering capabilities to visualize its deformations and interactions within the scene.

3. **Real-time Interaction**: Allow user interactions or scripted events to affect the soft body, such as applying external forces or constraints.

Soft body simulation with finite elements in Vulkan enables the creation of highly realistic deformable objects and materials, adding depth and realism to computer graphics applications. Whether it's simulating cloth, character deformations, or medical soft tissues, the integration of soft body physics into Vulkan-based rendering pipelines contributes to more immersive and visually compelling experiences.

Section 5.4: Hair and Fur Simulation

HAIR AND FUR SIMULATION is a specialized area of computer graphics that focuses on simulating the behavior of hair strands and fur fibers. This simulation is crucial for creating realistic and dynamic hair and fur in characters and creatures in movies, games, and animations. In this section, we will delve into hair and fur simulation, its applications, numerical methods, and how it can be implemented in real-time rendering using Vulkan.

Understanding Hair and Fur Simulation

HAIR AND FUR SIMULATION involves modeling the complex behavior of individual hair strands or fur fibers and their interactions with one another and the environment. The simulation takes into account physical properties such as elasticity, bending, and friction, as well as external forces like gravity and wind. The goal is to create visually convincing animations and renderings of hair and fur.

Key Components of Hair and Fur Simulation:

1. **Strand Representation**: Hair and fur are represented as a collection of individual strands, each composed of multiple segments or control points.
2. **Physical Properties**: Each strand has physical properties such as length, thickness, stiffness, and mass that determine its behavior.

3. **Forces and Interactions**: External forces like gravity and wind, as well as interactions with surfaces and other strands, affect the behavior of hair and fur.
4. **Collision Detection**: Detecting collisions with objects, characters, or the environment is essential for realistic simulations.

Applications of Hair and Fur Simulation

HAIR AND FUR SIMULATION finds applications in various domains:

1. **Character Animation**: It's used to create realistic hair and fur for characters in movies, games, and animations.
2. **Wildlife Simulation**: Simulating fur is essential for creating lifelike animals and creatures in nature documentaries and video games.
3. **Cosmetics and Fashion**: The fashion industry uses hair simulation to showcase hairstyles and products in virtual fashion shows.
4. **Product Visualization**: Hair and fur simulation can enhance the visualization of products like clothing, furniture, and textiles.

Numerical Methods for Hair and Fur Simulation

SIMULATING HAIR AND fur involves solving equations that describe the behavior of individual strands. Common numerical methods include:

1. **Mass-Spring Systems**: Modeling hair as a collection of masses connected by springs allows for efficient simulations of bending and deformation.
2. **Particle-Based Methods**: Representing hair strands as

particles with constraints enables realistic simulations of strand interactions and collisions.

3. **Continuum Mechanics**: Hair can be treated as a continuous medium, and continuum mechanics equations can describe its deformation and behavior.

4. **Implicit Integration**: Numerical integration methods like implicit Euler or implicit backward Euler are often used for stable simulations.

Implementing Hair and Fur Simulation in Vulkan

INTEGRATING HAIR AND fur simulation into Vulkan-based applications involves several steps:

1. **Strand Representation**: Create a representation of hair and fur strands, including control points, physical properties, and initial configurations.

2. **Physical Modeling**: Implement the physical behavior of hair and fur strands, including calculations for bending, stretching, and collisions.

3. **Time Integration**: Update the positions and deformations of hair and fur strands over time steps using numerical integration methods.

```
// Example Vulkan code for updating hair and fur strand positions
using implicit Euler method

void                UpdateHairStrandPositions(VkCommandBuffer
commandBuffer, HairStrand strand, float deltaTime) {

// Calculate forces and deformations for the strand

CalculateForcesAndDeformations(strand);

// Update strand positions using implicit Euler method
```

UpdatePositionsImplicitly(strand, deltaTime);

}

1. **Collision Detection and Resolution**: Implement collision detection algorithms to detect and respond to collisions between hair and fur strands and objects or surfaces in the scene.
2. **Rendering Integration**: Render the hair and fur strands using Vulkan's rendering capabilities to visualize their motion and appearance within the scene.
3. **Real-time Interaction**: Allow user interactions or scripted events to affect the hair and fur simulation, such as wind forces or grooming tools.

Hair and fur simulation in Vulkan empowers developers to create realistic and visually stunning characters, creatures, and objects with dynamic and convincing hair and fur. Whether it's for animating a character's flowing locks, creating lifelike animals, or showcasing virtual fashion, the integration of hair and fur physics into Vulkan-based rendering pipelines enhances the overall realism and appeal of computer graphics applications.

Section 5.5: Crowd Dynamics

CROWD DYNAMICS SIMULATION is a specialized area of computer graphics and artificial intelligence that focuses on simulating the behavior of large groups of virtual characters or entities, often referred to as crowds. This simulation is essential for creating realistic and dynamic crowd scenes in movies, video games, architectural visualizations, and other interactive applications. In this section, we will explore crowd dynamics simulation, its applications, numerical methods, and how it can be implemented in real-time rendering using Vulkan.

Understanding Crowd Dynamics Simulation

CROWD DYNAMICS SIMULATION involves modeling the movement, interactions, and behaviors of a large number of individual entities within a crowd. These entities can represent pedestrians, vehicles, animals, or any other objects that form a collective group. The simulation takes into account factors such as navigation, collision avoidance, group cohesion, and response to environmental stimuli.

Key Components of Crowd Dynamics Simulation:

1. **Entity Representation**: Each entity in the crowd is represented as an individual agent with attributes like position, velocity, and behavior rules.
2. **Navigation and Pathfinding**: Agents navigate within the environment, avoiding obstacles and following paths or waypoints.
3. **Behavior Rules**: Agents follow predefined behavior rules that dictate how they interact with each other and respond to external factors.
4. **Collision Avoidance**: Collision detection and avoidance algorithms ensure that agents do not collide with each other or obstacles.

Applications of Crowd Dynamics Simulation

CROWD DYNAMICS SIMULATION has numerous applications across various domains:

1. **Entertainment**: In video games and movies, it creates realistic crowds in urban environments, battle scenes, sports events, and more.
2. **Architectural Visualization**: Architects use crowd simulations to showcase how people move within and interact with buildings and public spaces.
3. **Urban Planning**: It aids in urban design and transportation planning by simulating pedestrian and vehicular traffic flows.
4. **Safety and Evacuation Planning**: Simulations are used to study crowd behavior during emergencies and plan safe evacuation routes.
5. **Training and Education**: Simulations can serve as training tools for emergency responders and event staff.

Numerical Methods for Crowd Dynamics Simulation

CROWD DYNAMICS SIMULATION relies on various numerical and algorithmic methods to model agent behavior and interactions:

1. **Agent-Based Modeling**: Each agent follows a set of rules that define its behavior, such as avoiding collisions, following paths, and responding to stimuli.
2. **Navigation Meshes**: The environment is often divided into a navigation mesh that guides agents in pathfinding and obstacle avoidance.
3. **Behavior Trees**: Behavior trees provide a hierarchical way to define agent behaviors and decision-making processes.
4. **Flocking Algorithms**: Flocking algorithms, like boids, simulate collective behavior by defining rules for alignment, separation, and cohesion among agents.

Implementing Crowd Dynamics Simulation in Vulkan

INTEGRATING CROWD DYNAMICS simulation into Vulkan-based applications involves several steps:

1. **Agent Representation**: Create a representation for individual agents in the crowd, including their positions, velocities, and behavior rules.
2. **Navigation and Pathfinding**: Implement navigation and pathfinding algorithms to guide agents through the environment while avoiding obstacles and other agents.
3. **Behavior Rules**: Define behavior rules that govern how agents interact with each other and respond to external factors, such as avoiding collisions and maintaining group cohesion.
4. **Collision Detection and Avoidance**: Implement collision detection and avoidance algorithms to ensure that agents do not collide with each other or obstacles.
5. **Rendering Integration**: Render the crowd of agents using Vulkan's rendering capabilities to visualize their movements and interactions within the scene.
6. **Real-time Interaction**: Allow user interactions or scripted events to affect the crowd simulation, such as changing agent behaviors or triggering events.

```
// Example Vulkan code for updating agent positions in a crowd simulation

void UpdateAgentPositions(VkCommandBuffer commandBuffer, CrowdAgent agent, float deltaTime) {

// Calculate agent movements based on behavior rules and pathfinding
```

```
CalculateAgentMovements(agent, deltaTime);

// Update agent positions using the calculated movements

UpdatePositions(agent, deltaTime);

}
```

Crowd dynamics simulation in Vulkan empowers developers to create immersive and realistic crowd scenes with dynamic and responsive behaviors. Whether it's populating a virtual city with pedestrians, simulating a bustling marketplace, or orchestrating large-scale battles, the integration of crowd dynamics into Vulkan-based rendering pipelines enhances the overall realism and interactivity of computer graphics applications.

Chapter 6: Volumetric and Holographic Rendering

Section 6.1: Introduction to Volumetrics

Volumetric rendering is a technique used in computer graphics to simulate and render three-dimensional volumes of data. Unlike traditional surface-based rendering, which deals with surfaces and polygons, volumetric rendering focuses on the visualization of the interior of objects or scenes. In this section, we'll explore the fundamentals of volumetric rendering and its applications within the context of Vulkan.

Understanding Volumetric Rendering

VOLUMETRIC RENDERING involves the generation of imagery from data that defines a volume. This data can represent various phenomena, such as:

- **Medical Imaging**: Volumetric rendering is widely used in the medical field to visualize and analyze complex 3D data obtained from techniques like CT scans and MRI.

- **Scientific Visualization**: Researchers use volumetric rendering to visualize and analyze scientific data, such as fluid simulations, weather simulations, and more.

- **Computer Graphics**: In computer graphics, volumetric rendering enables the creation of realistic fog, smoke, fire, clouds, and other atmospheric effects.

Key Concepts in Volumetric Rendering:

1. **Volume Data**: Volumetric rendering starts with volume data, which is typically a 3D grid of values representing properties like density, color, or opacity within the volume.
2. **Raycasting**: The most common technique for volumetric rendering is raycasting, where rays are cast through the volume data to determine how they interact with the volume, including absorption and scattering.
3. **Transfer Functions**: Transfer functions map data values to optical properties, allowing control over the appearance of the rendered volume.

Applications of Volumetric Rendering

VOLUMETRIC RENDERING finds applications in various fields:

- **Medical Imaging**: It helps visualize internal structures in 3D, aiding diagnosis and treatment planning.

- **Scientific Visualization**: Researchers use it to gain insights into complex scientific phenomena.

- **Special Effects**: In movies and games, volumetric rendering creates realistic smoke, fire, and other atmospheric effects.

- **Engineering**: Engineers use it to visualize and analyze data from simulations.

Implementing Volumetric Rendering in Vulkan

TO IMPLEMENT VOLUMETRIC rendering in Vulkan, you need to:

1. **Data Acquisition**: Obtain or generate volume data, which can come from sources like medical scans, simulations, or procedural generation.
2. **Data Representation**: Represent the volume data in a format suitable for GPU processing, such as 3D textures or compute buffers.
3. **Raycasting**: Implement raycasting shaders that simulate the path of light rays through the volume, accumulating color and opacity along the way.
4. **Transfer Functions**: Create transfer functions that map volume data values to optical properties, allowing you to control the appearance of the rendered volume.
5. **Volume Rendering Pipeline**: Set up a rendering pipeline in Vulkan that incorporates raycasting shaders and transfer functions.
6. **Interaction and Real-time Updates**: Implement user interaction and real-time updates if needed, allowing users to explore and interact with volumetric data.

```glsl
// Example Vulkan shader code for raycasting in volumetric rendering

#version 450

layout(set = 0, binding = 0, rgba8) uniform writeonly image3D g_outputImage;

void main() {

// Raycasting algorithm goes here

// Accumulate color and opacity along the ray

// Write the result to g_outputImage

}
```

Volumetric rendering in Vulkan opens up opportunities to create visually stunning and informative 3D visualizations. Whether it's visualizing complex scientific data, enhancing medical imaging, or adding realistic atmospheric effects to games and simulations, understanding volumetric rendering techniques can greatly enrich your graphics programming skills.

Section 6.2: Real-time Volumetric Shadows

REAL-TIME VOLUMETRIC shadows are a crucial component of immersive and realistic 3D graphics. They add depth and realism to scenes by simulating the interaction of light with volumes such as smoke, fog, and other participating media. In this section, we'll delve into the techniques and methods for achieving real-time volumetric shadows in Vulkan-based graphics applications.

Understanding Volumetric Shadows

VOLUMETRIC SHADOWS occur when light interacts with a volume, casting shadows within the volume itself and on other surfaces. For example, when sunlight passes through dense fog, it creates visible shadows within the fog and casts shadows on objects behind the fog. Achieving real-time volumetric shadows involves simulating these intricate light interactions efficiently.

Challenges in Real-time Volumetric Shadows:

1. **Complex Light Transport**: Volumetric shadows require simulating the complex transport of light within a participating medium. This involves modeling absorption, scattering, and emission of light.
2. **Performance**: Real-time applications demand efficient algorithms to compute volumetric shadows without

significant frame rate drops.

3. **Integration with Other Effects**: Volumetric shadows
    often need to be integrated with other rendering effects,
    such as global illumination and reflections.

Techniques for Real-time Volumetric Shadows

1. **Shadow Mapping**: One approach is to use shadow
    mapping techniques to render shadows from a light source.
    This involves rendering a shadow map from the light's
    perspective and then using it to determine which parts of
    the volume are in shadow.

2. **Voxel-based Approaches**: Voxel grids can represent the
    volume, and shadow information is stored in the voxels.
    Raymarching or raycasting techniques can then be used to
    determine shadow contributions along camera rays.

3. **Light Scattering**: For participating media like fog,
    simulating the scattering of light can create volumetric
    shadows. Techniques like the phase function and Henyey-
    Greenstein scattering can be used.

4. **Screen Space Techniques**: Some real-time volumetric
    shadow methods operate in screen space, using the depth
    buffer and screen-space raymarching to compute shadows
    efficiently.

Implementing Real-time Volumetric Shadows in Vulkan

TO IMPLEMENT REAL-TIME volumetric shadows in Vulkan,
you'll need to:

1. **Volume Representation**: Represent the participating
    volume, typically using a 3D texture or voxel grid.

2. **Shadow Map**: Render a shadow map from the light source's perspective.
3. **Light Transport**: Compute the interaction of light with the volume, considering absorption, scattering, and emission.
4. **Shadow Computation**: Determine which parts of the volume are in shadow by comparing the shadow map with the volume representation.
5. **Rendering Integration**: Integrate the volumetric shadows into your overall rendering pipeline, considering the interaction with other effects.
6. **Performance Optimization**: Optimize the algorithms for real-time performance, as volumetric shadows can be computationally intensive.

```glsl
// Example Vulkan shader code for real-time volumetric shadows

#version 450

layout(set = 0, binding = 0, rgba8) uniform writeonly image2D g_outputImage;

layout(set = 0, binding = 1) uniform sampler2DShadow g_shadowMap;

layout(set = 0, binding = 2) uniform sampler3D g_volumeTexture;

void main() {

// Perform raymarching through the volume

// Sample the shadow map and compute shadow contributions

// Accumulate the final color considering volumetric shadows

// Write the result to g_outputImage
```

}

Real-time volumetric shadows can enhance the visual quality and immersion of your graphics applications. Understanding the principles and techniques involved in simulating these shadows in Vulkan opens up possibilities for creating captivating and realistic scenes.

Section 6.3: Holographic Displays and Vulkan

HOLOGRAPHIC DISPLAYS have long been a staple of science fiction, but recent advancements in technology have brought us closer to making them a reality. These displays offer the promise of three-dimensional, volumetric images that can be viewed from different angles without the need for special glasses or headsets. In this section, we'll explore the intersection of holographic displays and the Vulkan graphics API.

Understanding Holographic Displays

HOLOGRAPHIC DISPLAYS work by creating a light field that simulates the way light interacts with objects in the real world. This allows for the creation of 3D images that appear to occupy physical space. Unlike traditional displays that project images onto flat surfaces, holographic displays aim to reproduce the natural behavior of light.

Key Characteristics of Holographic Displays:

1. **Parallax**: Holographic displays offer parallax, meaning viewers can see different perspectives of a 3D object as they move around it, just as they would with a physical object.

2. **Light Field**: These displays emit or reflect light in a way that mimics the behavior of real-world objects. This includes the ability to cast shadows and display highlights.
3. **Volumetric Depth**: Holographic images have true depth, allowing viewers to perceive objects as having volume and occupying space.

Challenges in Rendering for Holographic Displays

RENDERING FOR HOLOGRAPHIC displays presents unique challenges:

1. **Light Field Synthesis**: To create a convincing 3D image, the display needs to synthesize a light field that accurately represents the scene. This involves precise control over the direction, intensity, and color of light rays.
2. **Real-time Performance**: Achieving real-time rendering for holographic displays can be demanding, as it often involves complex computations for light field synthesis.
3. **Content Creation**: Creating content for holographic displays requires new tools and techniques, as traditional 2D or 3D content may not translate well.

Implementing Holographic Rendering in Vulkan

TO IMPLEMENT HOLOGRAPHIC rendering in Vulkan, you would typically follow these steps:

1. **Light Field Synthesis**: Develop algorithms and shaders for synthesizing the required light field. This may involve ray tracing or other advanced techniques.
2. **Rendering Pipeline**: Set up a rendering pipeline in Vulkan that incorporates the light field synthesis shaders.
3. **Content Creation**: Create or adapt content that takes

advantage of the holographic capabilities. This might involve creating 3D models with realistic materials and lighting.

4. **Interaction**: Implement user interaction and input mechanisms that allow viewers to explore and interact with the holographic content.

5. **Performance Optimization**: Optimize the rendering process for real-time performance, considering the computational demands of light field synthesis.

// Example Vulkan shader code for holographic rendering

#version 450

```
layout(set = 0, binding = 0, rgba8) uniform writeonly image2D g_outputImage;

void main() {

// Perform holographic rendering calculations here

// Synthesize the light field for the 3D scene

// Write the result to g_outputImage

}
```

Holographic displays have the potential to revolutionize the way we interact with digital content, from gaming and entertainment to education and design. Integrating Vulkan with holographic displays can bring us closer to achieving immersive, true-to-life 3D experiences.

Section 6.4: Holographic Shader Techniques

CREATING CONVINCING holographic visuals often requires specialized shader techniques that can simulate the unique properties of holographic displays. In this section, we'll explore some of the shader techniques and considerations when developing content for holographic displays in Vulkan.

Simulating Light Field Synthesis

HOLOGRAPHIC DISPLAYS aim to replicate the behavior of light rays as they interact with objects in the real world. This means that shaders for holographic displays must simulate the complex process of light field synthesis. Techniques for simulating light field synthesis include:

- **Ray Tracing**: Using ray tracing shaders to model the path of light rays as they interact with the 3D scene. This involves tracing rays from the viewer's perspective and computing their interactions with objects in the scene.

- **Volume Rendering**: Implementing volumetric rendering techniques that can produce the appearance of objects with depth and volume. This is essential for creating convincing 3D holographic visuals.

Handling Parallax

ONE OF THE KEY FEATURES of holographic displays is parallax, where viewers can perceive different perspectives of an object as they move around it. Shader techniques for handling parallax include:

- **View-dependent Rendering**: Adjusting the rendering based on the viewer's perspective to account for parallax. This may involve changing the viewpoint or altering the rendering process.

- **Dynamic Depth of Field**: Implementing dynamic depth of field effects to enhance the perception of depth and parallax. This can help in making objects appear more realistic in a holographic context.

Realistic Materials and Lighting

HOLOGRAPHIC DISPLAYS benefit from realistic materials and lighting effects. Shaders can simulate various materials and lighting scenarios to achieve convincing visuals. Techniques include:

- **Physically Based Rendering (PBR)**: Implementing PBR shaders that accurately model how light interacts with different materials, including factors like reflection, refraction, and specular highlights.

- **Global Illumination**: Simulating global illumination effects to achieve realistic indirect lighting. This can enhance the overall realism of holographic scenes.

Special Effects and Interaction

HOLOGRAPHIC DISPLAYS allow for unique special effects and interactive elements. Shaders can be used to create effects like:

- **Holographic Glows**: Implementing shader-based glows and auras around holographic objects to make them appear more ethereal and otherworldly.

- **Interactive Elements**: Developing shaders that respond to user interactions, such as touch or gestures, to create dynamic and engaging holographic experiences.

Performance Optimization

GIVEN THE COMPUTATIONAL demands of simulating complex light interactions and parallax, shader performance optimization is crucial for real-time holographic rendering. Techniques include:

- **Level of Detail (LOD)**: Implementing LOD techniques to reduce the complexity of shaders for objects that are farther from the viewer's perspective.

- **Shader Caching**: Caching shader results to avoid redundant calculations and improve rendering efficiency.

- **Parallelism**: Leveraging Vulkan's support for parallelism to distribute shader calculations across multiple GPU cores.

// Example Vulkan shader code for holographic rendering

#version 450

layout(set = 0, binding = 0, rgba8) uniform writeonly image2D g_outputImage;

layout(set = 0, binding = 1) uniform sampler2D g_depthTexture;

void main() {

// Perform holographic shader calculations here

// Simulate light field synthesis, parallax, materials, and lighting

// Write the final holographic result to g_outputImage

}

Developing shaders for holographic displays in Vulkan requires a deep understanding of the unique characteristics of holographic technology and the ability to simulate these characteristics effectively. By mastering these shader techniques, you can create immersive and captivating holographic experiences.

Section 6.5: Interactive Volumetric Data Visualization

INTERACTIVE VOLUMETRIC data visualization is a powerful application of Vulkan graphics that allows users to explore and interact with complex 3D datasets. Whether it's medical imaging, scientific simulations, or architectural modeling, Vulkan provides the tools needed to visualize volumetric data effectively.

Understanding Volumetric Data

VOLUMETRIC DATA TYPICALLY consists of a 3D grid of values, where each value represents a property such as density, temperature, or concentration at a specific point in space. This data can be obtained from various sources, including medical scans, simulations, or 3D scanning technologies.

Key Characteristics of Volumetric Data:

1. **3D Grid**: Volumetric data is inherently three-dimensional, which means it has width, height, and depth, making it different from 2D images.
2. **Scalar or Vector Fields**: Data points in the grid can represent scalar values (e.g., temperature) or vector values

(e.g., velocity vectors).

3. **Real-world Scale**: Volumetric data is often associated with real-world scale, making it suitable for various applications like medical diagnoses and simulations.

Techniques for Interactive Volumetric Data Visualization

1. **Volume Rendering**: Volume rendering techniques allow you to convert volumetric data into images that convey the 3D structure and properties. This involves algorithms like ray casting, texture-based rendering, and GPU-based ray marching.
2. **Transfer Functions**: Transfer functions map scalar values to color and opacity, enabling the highlighting of specific features or structures within the volume.
3. **3D Widgets**: Implementing 3D widgets or controls that allow users to manipulate the viewing perspective, slice through the data, or adjust rendering parameters interactively.
4. **Real-time Interaction**: Enabling real-time interaction with the volume data, such as zooming, panning, and selecting regions of interest.
5. **Multi-resolution Rendering**: Utilizing multi-resolution rendering techniques to optimize performance when dealing with large volumetric datasets.

Implementing Interactive Volumetric Visualization in Vulkan

TO IMPLEMENT INTERACTIVE volumetric visualization in Vulkan, consider the following steps:

1. **Data Loading**: Load volumetric data from your data source. This could involve reading medical DICOM files, importing simulation results, or using 3D scanning data.
2. **Data Preprocessing**: Preprocess the data as needed, such as resampling, filtering, or normalizing to prepare it for rendering.
3. **Rendering Pipeline**: Set up a rendering pipeline in Vulkan that includes shaders and techniques for volume rendering. This may involve ray casting, shader-based transfer functions, and real-time interaction handling.
4. **User Interaction**: Implement user interaction mechanisms to allow users to explore and interact with the volumetric data. This may include camera controls, slicing, and parameter adjustments.
5. **Optimization**: Optimize the rendering process for real-time performance, especially if dealing with large datasets. Techniques like level of detail (LOD) and data compression may be useful.

```glsl
// Example Vulkan shader code for interactive volumetric rendering

#version 450

layout(set = 0, binding = 0, rgba8) uniform writeonly image2D g_outputImage;

layout(set = 0, binding = 1) uniform sampler3D g_volumeTexture;

void main() {

// Perform interactive volumetric rendering calculations here

// Apply transfer functions, handle user interactions, and render the volume
```

// Write the final result to g_outputImage

}

Interactive volumetric data visualization in Vulkan opens up possibilities for applications in various fields, from medical imaging and scientific simulations to immersive virtual environments. By leveraging Vulkan's capabilities, you can create engaging and informative 3D experiences that allow users to explore and understand complex volumetric datasets.

Chapter 7: Advanced Real-time Ray Tracing

Section 7.1: Implementing Path Tracing

Path tracing is a rendering technique used in computer graphics to simulate the behavior of light as it interacts with objects in a scene. Unlike traditional rasterization, which follows a forward rendering approach, path tracing is a global illumination technique that simulates the path of individual rays of light as they bounce around the scene, contributing to the final image. In this section, we will explore the implementation of path tracing in Vulkan, leveraging the capabilities of ray tracing.

Understanding Path Tracing

PATH TRACING FOLLOWS a stochastic process where rays of light are traced backward from the camera into the scene. These rays undergo multiple interactions, such as reflection, refraction, and diffuse scattering, until they reach a light source or are terminated after a certain number of bounces. The process is inherently recursive, as each interaction spawns new rays that contribute to the final pixel color.

Key Concepts in Path Tracing:

1. **Ray Generation**: The path tracing algorithm begins with the generation of primary rays from the camera's viewpoint.
2. **Ray Intersection**: Primary rays are tested for intersections

with scene geometry. When an intersection occurs, the algorithm calculates secondary rays for reflection, refraction, or scattering.

3. **Multiple Bounces**: Rays continue to bounce around the scene, accumulating color information at each bounce. These bounces can be controlled to achieve the desired level of realism.

4. **Light Sampling**: To simulate global illumination, the algorithm also samples lights in the scene, contributing their radiance to the paths.

Implementing Path Tracing in Vulkan

TO IMPLEMENT PATH TRACING in Vulkan, you would typically follow these steps:

1. **Ray Tracing Pipeline**: Set up a ray tracing pipeline in Vulkan, which includes ray generation, ray intersection, and closest hit shaders. These shaders define the behavior of rays and how they interact with scene geometry.

2. **Ray Generation**: Write the ray generation shader, responsible for generating primary rays and initializing the ray tracing process.

3. **Ray Intersection**: Implement the ray intersection shader, which calculates ray-object intersections and determines the type of interaction (e.g., reflection, refraction) to continue the path.

4. **Multiple Bounces**: Create shaders for multiple bounces of rays, which recursively trace secondary rays based on the interactions. Care must be taken to avoid infinite recursion.

5. **Light Sampling**: Incorporate light sampling techniques to simulate global illumination. This involves sampling light

sources in the scene and computing their contribution to the rays.

6. **Accumulation and Rendering**: Accumulate the color information at each bounce and render the final image using the ray tracing pipeline.

```glsl
// Example Vulkan shader code for path tracing

#version 460

layout(set = 0, binding = 0, rgba8) uniform writeonly image2D g_outputImage;

layout(set = 0, binding = 1) buffer g_sceneBuffer { /* scene data */ };

void main() {

// Ray generation shader

// Generate primary rays and initiate the path tracing process

// Trace rays, calculate intersections, and perform multiple bounces

// Accumulate color information and write the result to g_outputImage

}
```

Path tracing is computationally intensive, but it is capable of producing highly realistic images with accurate lighting and global illumination effects. Leveraging Vulkan's ray tracing capabilities, you can implement path tracing algorithms that achieve stunning visual quality and realism in your graphics applications.

Section 7.2: Photon Mapping

PHOTON MAPPING IS A global illumination technique used in computer graphics to simulate the indirect lighting in a scene accurately. It is especially valuable in achieving realistic lighting effects such as caustics, color bleeding, and soft shadows. In this section, we will delve into the concept of photon mapping and how to implement it in Vulkan.

Understanding Photon Mapping

PHOTON MAPPING OPERATES by tracing photons from light sources into the scene and then using a data structure called the photon map to efficiently compute the indirect lighting in the scene. The photon map stores information about the photons, including their positions, directions, colors, and energy. The algorithm consists of two main phases: photon tracing and photon gathering.

Key Concepts in Photon Mapping:

1. **Photon Tracing**: In this phase, photons are emitted from light sources and traced through the scene. Each photon undergoes multiple interactions, such as reflection and refraction, before being stored in the photon map when it hits a surface.
2. **Photon Gathering**: When rendering a pixel, the algorithm queries the photon map to estimate the indirect lighting contribution. It finds the nearby photons and combines their energy to compute the pixel's final color.

Implementing Photon Mapping in Vulkan

TO IMPLEMENT PHOTON mapping in Vulkan, you can follow these steps:

1. **Photon Tracing**: Create a Vulkan ray tracing pipeline to trace photons from light sources into the scene. Implement ray generation, ray-object intersection, and photon storage in the closest hit shader.

2. **Photon Gathering**: When rendering a pixel, perform a query on the photon map to find nearby photons. Estimate the indirect lighting contribution by combining the energy of these photons.

3. **Photon Map Construction**: During photon tracing, store the photons in a data structure optimized for efficient queries, such as a kd-tree or a photon map grid.

4. **Caustics**: Photon mapping excels at simulating caustics, which are focused and intensified light patterns. Implement caustic photon tracing specifically for scenes with caustic effects.

5. **Multiple Bounces**: You can extend the photon mapping algorithm to handle multiple bounces to capture complex indirect lighting interactions.

6. **Optimization**: Photon mapping can be computationally expensive. Implement optimization techniques such as importance sampling, Russian roulette, and photon mapping with progressive refinement to improve performance.

// Example Vulkan shader code for photon mapping

#version 460

layout(set = 0, binding = 0, rgba8) uniform writeonly image2D g_outputImage;

layout(set = 0, binding = 1) buffer g_sceneBuffer { */* scene data */* };

layout(set = 0, binding = 2) buffer g_photonBuffer { /* *photon map data* */ };

void main() {

// Ray generation shader for photon tracing

// Trace photons from light sources into the scene

// Implement photon gathering to estimate indirect lighting

// Store and query photons in the photon map

// Compute the final color for the pixel and write it to g_outputImage

}

Photon mapping is a powerful technique for achieving realistic and complex lighting effects in computer graphics. By implementing it in Vulkan, you can create scenes with accurate indirect lighting, caustics, and soft shadows, enhancing the visual quality of your graphics applications.

Section 7.3: Radiance and Irradiance Caching

RADIANCE AND IRRADIANCE caching are techniques used in computer graphics to efficiently compute global illumination in a scene. These techniques leverage precomputed data structures to accelerate the rendering process while maintaining high-quality indirect lighting effects. In this section, we will explore radiance and irradiance caching and how to implement them in Vulkan.

Understanding Radiance and Irradiance Caching

GLOBAL ILLUMINATION is a computationally intensive process that simulates the indirect lighting in a scene, including effects like color bleeding, soft shadows, and reflections. Radiance and irradiance caching aim to reduce the computational cost by storing and reusing lighting information.

Key Concepts:

1. **Radiance**: Radiance represents the amount of light energy emitted or reflected by a surface in a specific direction. It is commonly used to compute direct and indirect lighting.
2. **Irradiance**: Irradiance represents the incoming light energy received by a surface from all directions. It is used to compute the indirect lighting at a point.
3. **Radiance Caching**: Radiance caching stores radiance values at specific points in the scene, allowing for fast lookup during rendering. When a ray intersects a cached point, the stored radiance is used, reducing the need for costly ray tracing calculations.
4. **Irradiance Caching**: Irradiance caching precomputes irradiance values at specific points on surfaces. During rendering, irradiance values are interpolated between cache points to estimate indirect lighting efficiently.

Implementing Radiance and Irradiance Caching in Vulkan

TO IMPLEMENT RADIANCE and irradiance caching in Vulkan, you can follow these steps:

1. **Radiance Caching:**

– Create a data structure to store radiance values at selected points in the scene, such as a 3D grid or sparse voxel octree.

– During rendering, when a ray intersects a cached point, use the stored radiance value to contribute to the final pixel color.

1. **Irradiance Caching**:

– Precompute irradiance values at specific points on surfaces. This can be done offline or during scene setup.

– During rendering, when shading a point on a surface, interpolate irradiance values from nearby cache points to estimate indirect lighting efficiently.

1. **Multiple Bounces**: Extend the caching techniques to handle multiple bounces to capture complex indirect lighting interactions.
2. **Cache Updates**: Implement cache updates to adapt to dynamic scenes or changes in lighting conditions.

// Example Vulkan shader code for radiance and irradiance caching

#version 460

```
layout(set = 0, binding = 0, rgba8) uniform writeonly image2D g_outputImage;

layout(set = 0, binding = 1) buffer g_sceneBuffer { /* scene data */ };

layout(set = 0, binding = 2) buffer g_radianceCache { /* radiance cache data */ };
```

layout(set = 0, binding = 3) buffer g_irradianceCache { /* *irradiance cache data* */ };

void main() {

// *Ray tracing or rasterization shader*

// *Implement radiance and irradiance caching techniques*

// *Look up radiance values or interpolate irradiance values as needed*

// *Compute the final color for the pixel and write it to g_outputImage*

}

Radiance and irradiance caching strike a balance between rendering speed and visual quality, making them valuable tools for achieving global illumination in real-time or interactive graphics applications. By incorporating these techniques into Vulkan-based rendering pipelines, you can enhance the realism and efficiency of your scenes' lighting.

Section 7.4: Real-time Caustics

REAL-TIME CAUSTICS are a visually stunning lighting phenomenon that occurs when light rays are refracted or reflected by curved surfaces, creating intricate and dynamic patterns of light and shadow. Caustics are often seen in scenes with water, glass, or other transparent materials. In this section, we will explore the techniques for simulating real-time caustics in Vulkan.

Understanding Caustics

CAUSTICS ARE A RESULT of the concentration of light energy in certain areas due to the focusing or scattering of light rays. They can be categorized into two main types:

1. **Refractive Caustics**: These caustics occur when light passes through a refractive medium, such as water or glass. The bending of light rays at the interface between air and the medium causes caustic patterns on surfaces.
2. **Reflective Caustics**: Reflective caustics are created when light reflects off curved or reflective surfaces, like metal or mirrors. The curvature of the surface concentrates light energy at specific points.

Simulating caustics accurately requires the tracing of a large number of rays, which can be computationally expensive. Therefore, efficient algorithms and techniques are essential for real-time rendering.

Implementing Real-time Caustics in Vulkan

TO IMPLEMENT REAL-TIME caustics in Vulkan, consider the following steps:

1. **Ray Tracing or Rasterization**: Decide whether to use ray tracing or rasterization for simulating caustics. Ray tracing allows for more accurate caustic effects but may be computationally intensive. Rasterization can provide real-time performance but with some simplification.
2. **Light Source Modeling**: Define the light sources responsible for generating caustics. For refractive caustics, consider point or area lights underwater. For reflective caustics, model the light sources and their positions.
3. **Ray Tracing (Refractive Caustics)**:

– Implement ray tracing to simulate the bending of light rays as they pass through refractive materials.

– Trace rays from the light sources and calculate their interactions with the refractive surfaces.

– Accumulate the caustic patterns on receiving surfaces, such as the ocean floor.

1. **Rasterization (Reflective Caustics):**

– For reflective caustics, you can achieve real-time performance through rasterization.

– Implement techniques like screen-space reflections (SSR) or reflective shadow maps (RSM) to capture reflective caustics.

1. **Optimization Techniques**: Employ optimization techniques such as importance sampling, photon mapping, or screen-space techniques to reduce the computational cost of simulating caustics.
2. **Dynamic Scenes**: Consider how to handle dynamic scenes or moving light sources, which may require updates to the caustic simulation in real-time.

```glsl
// Example Vulkan shader code for real-time caustics

#version 460

layout(set = 0, binding = 0, rgba8) uniform writeonly image2D g_outputImage;

layout(set = 0, binding = 1) buffer g_sceneBuffer { /* scene data */ };

void main() {

// Ray tracing or rasterization shader
```

// Implement real-time caustic simulation techniques

// Trace rays for refractive caustics or use rasterization for reflective caustics

// Accumulate the caustic patterns on surfaces and compute the final color

}

Real-time caustics add a level of realism and visual appeal to scenes with transparent or reflective materials. By implementing these techniques in Vulkan-based graphics applications, you can create captivating and dynamic lighting effects that enhance the overall visual quality of your renders.

Section 7.5: Noise Reduction Techniques

NOISE REDUCTION IS a critical aspect of real-time ray tracing and global illumination rendering techniques, as noise in rendered images can significantly degrade visual quality. Noise appears as unwanted graininess or speckles in images and is a result of sampling limitations and Monte Carlo integration used in ray tracing. In this section, we will explore various noise reduction techniques that can be applied to improve the quality of ray-traced or global illumination images in Vulkan-based rendering pipelines.

Understanding Image Noise

IMAGE NOISE CAN MANIFEST in different forms, including high-frequency noise, low-frequency noise, and temporal noise:

1. **High-Frequency Noise**: This noise appears as small, fine details that flicker from frame to frame. It often results from insufficient ray sampling and can be visually

distracting.

2. **Low-Frequency Noise**: Low-frequency noise creates large-scale patterns or blotches in an image. It can occur when indirect lighting is not well-distributed.

3. **Temporal Noise**: Temporal noise refers to noise that changes from frame to frame in an animation. It can be particularly problematic in real-time applications.

Noise Reduction Techniques

TO REDUCE NOISE IN ray-traced or global illumination images, consider the following techniques:

1. **Supersampling**: Increase the number of rays per pixel by supersampling. Techniques like jittered or adaptive sampling can help distribute rays more effectively.

2. **Filtering**: Apply image-space filtering techniques like bilateral filtering or Gaussian blur to smooth out noise while preserving image details.

3. **Denoising Algorithms**: Use denoising algorithms, such as AI-based denoising or spatial-temporal filtering, to remove noise from images. These algorithms can be implemented as post-processing steps.

4. **Importance Sampling**: Implement importance sampling techniques to sample rays more intelligently, focusing on regions with high lighting variability.

5. **Temporal Accumulation**: For animations, accumulate samples over multiple frames and apply temporal reprojection to reduce flickering noise.

6. **Adaptive Sampling**: Implement adaptive sampling strategies that allocate more rays to noisy or challenging areas in the scene.

```
// Example Vulkan shader code for noise reduction

#version 460

layout(set = 0, binding = 0, rgba8) uniform writeonly image2D
g_outputImage;

layout(set = 0, binding = 1) buffer g_sceneBuffer { /* scene data */ };

void main() {

// Ray tracing shader

// Implement noise reduction techniques, such as supersampling or
filtering

// Apply denoising algorithms as needed

// Temporal accumulation for animations can also be employed

}
```

The choice of noise reduction technique depends on the specific requirements of your application, including performance constraints and desired visual quality. Combining multiple techniques and experimenting with different settings can help achieve the best balance between real-time performance and noise reduction in Vulkan-based rendering systems.

Chapter 8: Realistic Atmospheric and Weather Effects

Section 8.1: Atmospheric Scattering

Atmospheric scattering is a crucial component of rendering realistic outdoor environments in computer graphics. It simulates the interaction of light with various particles and gases in the Earth's atmosphere, resulting in effects like aerial perspective, color shifts, and the scattering of sunlight. In this section, we will delve into the principles of atmospheric scattering and discuss how to implement it in Vulkan-based rendering systems.

The Physics of Atmospheric Scattering

TO ACHIEVE CONVINCING atmospheric scattering, it's essential to understand the underlying physics. Several factors contribute to this phenomenon:

1. **Rayleigh Scattering**: Rayleigh scattering occurs when shorter wavelengths of light (blue and violet) are scattered more than longer wavelengths (red and yellow). This is responsible for the blue appearance of the sky and the reddish hues during sunsets and sunrises.

2. **Mie Scattering**: Mie scattering involves larger particles, like dust and water droplets, scattering light more uniformly in all directions. This contributes to the whiteness of clouds.

3. **Aerial Perspective**: Objects at a distance appear less distinct and have a bluish tint due to the scattering of light

by atmospheric particles. This effect is known as aerial perspective and is crucial for creating depth in outdoor scenes.

Implementing Atmospheric Scattering

TO IMPLEMENT ATMOSPHERIC scattering in Vulkan, consider the following steps:

1. **Sky Model**: Define a sky model that simulates the scattering behavior of different wavelengths of light. This model should consider factors like Rayleigh and Mie scattering, the density of atmospheric particles, and the sun's position in the sky.
2. **Scattering Equations**: Implement the scattering equations that describe the interaction of light with the atmosphere. These equations determine the direction and intensity of scattered light at each point in the scene.
3. **Integration**: Integrate the scattering equations along the path of each ray of light as it travels through the atmosphere. This is typically done using numerical integration techniques like the discrete ordinate method (DOM) or the single scattering approximation.
4. **Color Rendering**: Calculate the final color of each pixel in the image by considering the contributions of scattered light from various directions and wavelengths. This involves spectral integration and color blending.
5. **Performance Optimization**: Atmospheric scattering can be computationally expensive. Employ techniques like precomputed atmospheric scattering tables or screen-space approximations to improve performance.

// Example Vulkan shader code for atmospheric scattering

#version 460

layout(set = 0, binding = 0, rgba8) uniform writeonly image2D g_outputImage;

layout(set = 0, binding = 1) buffer g_sceneBuffer { /* *scene data* */ };

void main() {

// *Ray tracing or rasterization shader*

// *Implement atmospheric scattering calculations*

// *Consider Rayleigh and Mie scattering, aerial perspective, and sun position*

// *Perform spectral integration for accurate color rendering*

}

Atmospheric scattering is a vital component of rendering realistic outdoor scenes, including skies, sunsets, and sunrises. By understanding the physics behind it and implementing the necessary calculations in Vulkan shaders, you can create visually stunning and immersive environments in your graphics applications.

Section 8.2: Real-time Cloud Simulation

REALISTIC CLOUD SIMULATION is a key element in creating immersive outdoor environments in computer graphics. It adds depth, atmosphere, and visual interest to scenes. In this section, we will explore techniques for real-time cloud simulation in Vulkan-based rendering systems.

Challenges in Cloud Simulation

SIMULATING CLOUDS CONVINCINGLY in real-time graphics presents several challenges:

1. **Performance**: Real-time cloud simulation can be computationally expensive. Achieving a balance between visual quality and performance is crucial.
2. **Volume Representation**: Representing clouds as 3D volumes with complex shapes and structures requires efficient data structures and algorithms.
3. **Light Interaction**: Clouds interact with light in various ways, including scattering, absorption, and transmission. Simulating these interactions accurately is essential for realistic rendering.

Techniques for Real-time Cloud Simulation

TO SIMULATE CLOUDS in real-time using Vulkan, consider the following techniques:

1. **Volumetric Representation**: Represent clouds as volumetric data structures, such as 3D grids or signed distance fields. This allows for efficient manipulation and rendering.
2. **Noise-based Generation**: Use noise functions, such as Perlin noise or simplex noise, to generate cloud shapes and textures. These functions can create the puffy, organic appearance of clouds.
3. **Dynamic Evolution**: Animate cloud formations by perturbing the volumetric data over time. This creates the illusion of cloud movement and evolution.
4. **Light Scattering**: Implement light scattering algorithms to simulate how clouds interact with sunlight. This involves

computing the color and intensity of scattered light.

5. **Shadowing and Self-shadowing**: Consider how clouds cast shadows on the ground and on other parts of the scene. Self-shadowing within the cloud volume is also important for realism.

6. **Noise Animation**: Animate the noise functions used for cloud generation to give the appearance of dynamic, turbulent clouds.

```glsl
// Example Vulkan shader code for real-time cloud simulation

#version 460

layout(set = 0, binding = 0, rgba8) uniform writeonly image2D g_outputImage;

layout(set = 0, binding = 1) buffer g_sceneBuffer { /* scene data */ };

void main() {

// Ray tracing or rasterization shader

// Implement real-time cloud simulation

// Use noise functions for cloud generation and animate them for realism

// Compute light scattering and handle shadowing effects

}
```

Real-time cloud simulation is a complex yet rewarding aspect of computer graphics. By using volumetric representations, noise-based generation, and sophisticated shading techniques, you can create visually stunning cloudscapes that enhance the realism and atmosphere of your Vulkan-based rendering projects.

Section 8.3: Dynamic Weather Systems

DYNAMIC WEATHER SYSTEMS play a significant role in creating immersive and ever-changing virtual worlds in computer graphics. These systems simulate various weather conditions like rain, snow, fog, and wind, adding realism and diversity to outdoor scenes. In this section, we will explore the implementation of dynamic weather systems in Vulkan-based rendering pipelines.

Importance of Dynamic Weather

DYNAMIC WEATHER SYSTEMS enhance the visual appeal and realism of virtual environments by introducing the following elements:

1. **Atmospheric Variation**: Changing weather conditions create variations in lighting, visibility, and mood, which contribute to a more engaging and believable world.
2. **Interactivity**: Dynamic weather allows for interactive experiences where weather conditions affect gameplay or user interaction. For example, rain may make surfaces slippery, affecting character movement.
3. **Aesthetics**: Weather effects like falling snow or rain can significantly improve the aesthetics of scenes, making them visually captivating.

Implementing Dynamic Weather

TO IMPLEMENT DYNAMIC weather in Vulkan-based graphics applications, consider the following steps:

1. **Weather Models**: Create weather models that define the parameters and behavior of different weather conditions. These models should include parameters like precipitation

rate, wind speed, cloud cover, and temperature.

2. **Particle Systems**: Simulate weather phenomena using particle systems. For example, raindrops or snowflakes can be represented as particles that move through the scene and interact with objects.

3. **Shading and Rendering**: Implement shaders and rendering techniques that depict weather effects. Rain, for instance, can be rendered as transparent streaks, and snowflakes can be rendered with appropriate reflections and refractions.

4. **Interactivity**: Integrate weather systems with the game or simulation logic to ensure that weather conditions affect the virtual world and gameplay elements. For example, rain may trigger puddle formation or affect sound propagation.

5. **Transitions**: Smoothly transition between different weather conditions to avoid abrupt changes that break immersion. Implement gradual changes in weather parameters over time.

```glsl
// Example Vulkan shader code for dynamic weather effects

#version 460

layout(set = 0, binding = 0, rgba8) uniform writeonly image2D g_outputImage;

layout(set = 0, binding = 1) buffer g_sceneBuffer { /* scene data */ };

void main() {

// Ray tracing or rasterization shader

// Implement dynamic weather effects, such as rain or snow

// Simulate particles and their interactions with the scene
```

// Adjust lighting and shading to match the current weather condition

}

Dynamic weather systems add depth and realism to virtual worlds. By simulating weather phenomena, integrating them with gameplay, and smoothly transitioning between conditions, you can create immersive experiences that respond dynamically to changing weather patterns in Vulkan-based graphics applications.

Section 8.4: Natural Phenomena (e.g., Rainbows, Aurora)

IN COMPUTER GRAPHICS, simulating natural phenomena like rainbows and auroras can add a touch of magic and wonder to virtual worlds. These phenomena are the result of complex interactions between light, particles, and the Earth's atmosphere. In this section, we will explore techniques for simulating natural phenomena in Vulkan-based rendering systems.

Simulating Rainbows

RAINBOWS ARE OPTICAL and meteorological phenomena that occur when sunlight is refracted, internally reflected, and dispersed in water droplets, resulting in a spectrum of colors appearing in the sky. To simulate rainbows:

1. **Light Refraction**: Implement the physics of light refraction as it enters and exits water droplets. This bending of light is responsible for the separation of colors in a rainbow.
2. **Internal Reflection**: Model the internal reflection of light inside the water droplets, which causes the light to bounce off the inner surface of the droplets.

3. **Spectrum Dispersion**: Simulate the dispersion of light into its constituent colors, creating the characteristic band of colors seen in a rainbow.

4. **Rendering**: Render the rainbow as a semi-circular or circular arc of colors in the sky, typically opposite the sun's position.

Simulating Auroras

AURORAS, SUCH AS THE Northern Lights (Aurora Borealis) and Southern Lights (Aurora Australis), are natural light displays caused by interactions between solar wind, the Earth's magnetic field, and the upper atmosphere. To simulate auroras:

1. **Solar Wind Interaction**: Model the interaction between solar wind particles and the Earth's magnetic field, which causes charged particles to enter the Earth's atmosphere near the polar regions.

2. **Ionization and Emission**: Simulate the ionization of gases in the upper atmosphere due to the incoming charged particles. This ionization results in the emission of light, creating the auroral glow.

3. **Color and Shape**: Render the auroras as vibrant, dynamic curtains of light that can vary in color, shape, and intensity.

4. **Movement**: Animate the movement of auroras to create the illusion of dynamic, shimmering curtains of light.

// Example Vulkan shader code for simulating natural phenomena

#version 460

layout(set = 0, binding = 0, rgba8) uniform writeonly image2D g_outputImage;

layout(set = 0, binding = 1) buffer g_sceneBuffer { /* *scene data* */ };

void main() {

// *Ray tracing or rasterization shader*

// *Implement the simulation of natural phenomena like rainbows or auroras*

// *Model the physics of light, particle interactions, and rendering*

// *Create visually captivating effects that enhance the virtual environment*

}

Simulating natural phenomena like rainbows and auroras requires a deep understanding of the underlying physics and careful implementation in shaders. By accurately modeling the interactions of light and particles, you can bring these awe-inspiring phenomena to life in your Vulkan-based rendering projects.

Section 8.5: Earth and Space Rendering Techniques

EARTH AND SPACE RENDERING are essential components of many computer graphics applications, including games, simulations, and educational software. Realistic depiction of Earth's surface, celestial bodies, and outer space environments can provide a visually captivating experience. In this section, we will explore techniques for rendering Earth and space in Vulkan-based graphics systems.

Earth Rendering Techniques

RENDERING THE EARTH'S surface realistically involves several key aspects:

1. **Terrain Generation**: Generate Earth's terrain, including mountains, valleys, oceans, and continents. Techniques like procedural generation or heightmaps can be used for this purpose.
2. **Texture Mapping**: Apply high-resolution satellite imagery as textures to the Earth's surface. These textures provide details such as land features, vegetation, and urban areas.
3. **Atmospheric Scattering**: Implement realistic atmospheric scattering models to accurately depict the Earth's atmosphere. This affects the color of the sky and the appearance of distant objects.
4. **Day-Night Cycle**: Create a dynamic day-night cycle with appropriate lighting and shadowing. This involves adjusting the position and intensity of sunlight as the virtual sun moves across the sky.
5. **Cloud Simulation**: As mentioned in previous sections, simulate dynamic cloud cover to enhance the Earth's appearance and realism.

Space Rendering Techniques

RENDERING SPACE ENVIRONMENTS can be equally challenging and rewarding:

1. **Celestial Bodies**: Render celestial bodies like stars, planets, moons, and asteroids. These objects should have accurate positions, sizes, and appearances.
2. **Nebulas and Galaxies**: Simulate nebulae, galaxies, and other cosmic phenomena using procedural techniques or high-resolution textures.
3. **Lighting Models**: Implement physically based lighting models for space environments, considering factors like starlight, planetshine, and the absence of atmosphere.

4. **Astronomical Phenomena**: Simulate astronomical events such as eclipses, meteor showers, and cometary appearances. These events can add interactivity and educational value.

5. **Spacecraft and Satellites**: Render spacecraft, satellites, and space stations if the application involves space exploration or science fiction themes.

// Example Vulkan shader code for Earth and space rendering

#version 460

layout(set = 0, binding = 0, rgba8) uniform writeonly image2D g_outputImage;

layout(set = 0, binding = 1) buffer g_sceneBuffer { */* scene data */* };

void main() {

// Ray tracing or rasterization shader

// Implement rendering techniques for Earth and space environments

// Consider terrain generation, texture mapping, atmospheric scattering,

// celestial body rendering, and lighting models for realism.

}

Rendering Earth and space environments requires a combination of techniques, including terrain generation, texture mapping, lighting models, and atmospheric scattering. By carefully implementing these techniques in Vulkan-based graphics systems, you can create visually stunning and immersive virtual worlds that depict the beauty of our planet and the mysteries of the cosmos.

Chapter 9: Hardware and Driver Deep Dive

In this chapter, we will embark on a journey into the depths of graphics hardware and its interaction with graphics drivers. Understanding the architecture and behavior of GPUs (Graphics Processing Units) and the role of graphics drivers is crucial for optimizing and achieving high-performance graphics rendering in Vulkan-based applications.

Section 9.1: Understanding Graphics Hardware Architecture

TO FULLY LEVERAGE THE power of Vulkan and achieve optimal performance, it's essential to comprehend the architecture of modern graphics hardware. GPUs have evolved significantly over the years, becoming highly parallel processors capable of handling complex rendering tasks. Here, we'll delve into the key aspects of graphics hardware architecture:

Parallel Processing Units:

MODERN GPUS CONSIST of thousands of processing cores, grouped into Streaming Multiprocessors (SMs) or Compute Units (CUs). Each SM or CU can execute multiple threads concurrently. Understanding how to effectively distribute rendering tasks across these cores is essential for achieving parallelism and performance.

Memory Hierarchy:

GRAPHICS HARDWARE INCLUDES various levels of memory, such as registers, shared memory, and global memory. Optimizing memory access patterns and utilizing fast, on-chip memory effectively can significantly boost rendering performance.

Shader Execution:

SHADERS ARE THE HEART of GPU rendering. Familiarizing yourself with different shader types, such as vertex shaders, fragment shaders, and compute shaders, and their execution models is crucial. We'll explore how to write efficient shaders that make the best use of available resources.

Pipelines and Stages:

GRAPHICS RENDERING involves multiple stages, including vertex processing, rasterization, and fragment processing. Understanding how these stages work together and optimizing data flow between them is essential for achieving high frame rates.

Graphics APIs:

GRAPHICS APIS LIKE Vulkan provide a low-level interface to interact with GPUs. Understanding how to use Vulkan effectively to harness the power of modern graphics hardware is a core part of this chapter.

Profiling and Analysis:

WE'LL EXPLORE TOOLS and techniques for profiling and analyzing the performance of your graphics applications on various GPUs. Profiling can help identify bottlenecks and areas for optimization.

// Example code for querying GPU information using Vulkan

VkPhysicalDevice physicalDevice;

vkEnumeratePhysicalDevices(instance, &physicalDeviceCount, &physicalDevice);

VkPhysicalDeviceProperties deviceProperties;

vkGetPhysicalDeviceProperties(physicalDevice, &deviceProperties);

This section will provide you with a solid foundation in understanding the architecture of graphics hardware. Armed with this knowledge, you'll be better equipped to optimize your Vulkan applications and achieve exceptional graphics performance.

Section 9.2: Driver Internals and Optimization

GRAPHICS DRIVERS PLAY a critical role in the interaction between your Vulkan-based application and the underlying hardware. In this section, we will dive into the internals of graphics drivers, understanding their function, and exploring optimization strategies to ensure your application runs efficiently.

The Role of Graphics Drivers:

GRAPHICS DRIVERS ACT as a bridge between your application and the GPU hardware. They translate Vulkan API calls into commands that the GPU can understand and execute. Understanding how drivers work internally can help you optimize your code.

Command Buffer Generation:

GRAPHICS DRIVERS ARE responsible for generating command buffers, which contain a sequence of commands for the GPU to execute. These commands include drawing instructions, memory transfers, and synchronization operations. Optimizing your Vulkan API usage can lead to more efficient command buffer generation.

Resource Management:

DRIVERS MANAGE GPU resources such as buffers, textures, and shader programs. Efficient resource management involves allocating and deallocating resources appropriately, minimizing redundant memory transfers, and reusing resources when possible.

Synchronization and Multithreading:

GRAPHICS DRIVERS MUST handle synchronization between the CPU and GPU to ensure data consistency. Understanding Vulkan's synchronization primitives and using them effectively can reduce synchronization overhead.

Driver Overhead:

GRAPHICS DRIVERS INTRODUCE some overhead due to the translation of Vulkan API calls into hardware-specific commands. Minimizing this overhead is crucial for achieving high performance. Vulkan's explicit nature allows you to control and optimize the driver overhead.

```
// Example Vulkan code for submitting a command buffer to the queue

VkSubmitInfo submitInfo = {};
```

```
submitInfo.sType                                    =
VK_STRUCTURE_TYPE_SUBMIT_INFO;

submitInfo.commandBufferCount = 1;

submitInfo.pCommandBuffers = &commandBuffer;

vkQueueSubmit(graphicsQueue,          1,          &submitInfo,
VK_NULL_HANDLE);

vkQueueWaitIdle(graphicsQueue);
```

Profiling and Debugging:

TO OPTIMIZE YOUR APPLICATION, it's essential to profile and debug it thoroughly. Vulkan provides tools and extensions for profiling, which allow you to analyze how your application interacts with the driver and the GPU.

Driver Updates:

GRAPHICS DRIVERS ARE regularly updated by GPU vendors to improve performance and fix issues. Keeping your drivers up to date can have a significant impact on the performance of your Vulkan applications.

Understanding graphics driver internals and optimizing your application's interaction with the driver can lead to substantial performance improvements. By minimizing unnecessary overhead, efficient resource management, and effective synchronization, you can ensure your Vulkan-based graphics application runs smoothly and efficiently on a variety of hardware configurations.

Section 9.3: Hardware Tessellation Techniques

HARDWARE TESSELLATION is a powerful feature available in modern GPUs that allows you to dynamically subdivide the geometry of 3D models, creating more detailed and smoother surfaces. In this section, we will explore hardware tessellation techniques in the context of Vulkan and how to harness this capability for improved graphics rendering.

Understanding Tessellation:

TESSELLATION INVOLVES dividing a coarse, low-polygon model into smaller, higher-polygon parts in real-time. This technique is particularly valuable for rendering complex surfaces with intricate details. Hardware tessellation typically consists of three main stages: tessellation control, tessellation evaluation, and primitive assembly.

Tessellation Control Shader (TCS):

THE TESSELLATION CONTROL shader is responsible for determining how much tessellation is required for each patch of geometry. It calculates control points and other parameters that guide the tessellation process.

Tessellation Evaluation Shader (TES):

THE TESSELLATION EVALUATION shader takes the control points generated by the TCS and computes the final vertex positions. It interpolates data across the tessellated surface and produces the vertices that make up the subdivided geometry.

Primitive Assembly:

ONCE THE TESSELLATED vertices are generated, the primitive assembly stage assembles them into triangles, lines, or points for rendering. These primitives are then sent to subsequent stages, including vertex shading and fragment shading.

Tessellation Factors:

IN VULKAN, YOU CAN control the tessellation level and other factors using tessellation control shader outputs. Adjusting these factors allows you to control the level of detail in the tessellated geometry dynamically.

// Example code snippet in GLSL for tessellation control shader

```glsl
layout(vertices = 4) out;

void main()
{
// Calculate tessellation levels
gl_TessLevelInner[0] = 4.0;

gl_TessLevelOuter[0] = 4.0;

gl_TessLevelOuter[1] = 4.0;

gl_TessLevelOuter[2] = 4.0;
}
```

Practical Applications:

HARDWARE TESSELLATION is commonly used in various graphics applications, including terrain rendering, character animation, and detailed object modeling. It allows you to achieve smooth, detailed surfaces without significantly increasing the model's polygon count, which can be a performance bottleneck.

Performance Considerations:

WHILE HARDWARE TESSELLATION can enhance graphics quality, it can also be demanding on GPU resources. It's crucial to strike a balance between tessellation levels and performance, especially on lower-end hardware.

Tessellation Culling:

TO FURTHER OPTIMIZE tessellation, you can implement culling techniques to skip the rendering of patches that are not visible or relevant to the current view. This reduces unnecessary work and improves rendering efficiency.

Understanding hardware tessellation and its integration into Vulkan can significantly enhance your ability to create detailed and visually appealing 3D graphics. By mastering tessellation control and evaluation shaders and optimizing tessellation factors, you can effectively leverage this GPU feature for a wide range of applications.

Section 9.4: Low-level GPU Programming

LOW-LEVEL GPU PROGRAMMING is a specialized skill that allows you to interact with the GPU hardware at a level closer to the metal. In this section, we will explore the advantages and challenges of low-level GPU programming in the context of Vulkan and how it can be leveraged for performance optimization and advanced rendering techniques.

Advantages of Low-level GPU Programming:

1. **Fine-grained Control:** Low-level GPU programming gives you precise control over how your application interacts with the GPU, enabling optimization for specific use cases.
2. **Performance Optimization:** By directly managing GPU resources and synchronization, you can fine-tune your application's performance and reduce overhead.
3. **Custom Rendering Techniques:** Low-level programming allows you to implement custom rendering techniques that may not be achievable through higher-level APIs.
4. **Cross-platform Compatibility:** Vulkan's low-level nature makes it suitable for cross-platform development, as it provides consistent control over GPU behavior across different devices and vendors.

Challenges of Low-level GPU Programming:

1. **Steep Learning Curve:** Low-level GPU programming can be complex and requires a deep understanding of GPU architecture and Vulkan's intricacies.
2. **Increased Development Time:** Writing low-level GPU code can be time-consuming compared to using higher-level APIs that abstract many details.
3. **Vendor-specific Code:** While Vulkan is cross-platform, writing low-level GPU code may still require vendor-specific optimizations to achieve the best performance on different GPUs.

Vulkan API for Low-level GPU Programming:

VULKAN'S DESIGN PHILOSOPHY emphasizes explicitness and control, making it well-suited for low-level GPU programming. Some key Vulkan features and concepts include:

- **Command Buffers:** Vulkan allows you to record and submit command buffers explicitly, enabling precise control over the execution of rendering commands.

- **Memory Management:** Vulkan provides mechanisms for managing GPU memory efficiently, including explicit memory allocation and deallocation.

- **Pipeline State Objects (PSOs):** PSOs in Vulkan define the rendering pipeline's state, allowing you to create custom rendering pipelines tailored to your needs.

```
// Example Vulkan code snippet for creating a pipeline object

VkPipelineLayoutCreateInfo pipelineLayoutInfo = {};

// Initialize and configure pipeline layout info...

VkPipelineLayout pipelineLayout;

vkCreatePipelineLayout(device, &pipelineLayoutInfo, nullptr, &pipelineLayout);
```

Use Cases for Low-level GPU Programming:

LOW-LEVEL GPU PROGRAMMING is particularly beneficial for tasks such as:

- Implementing custom rendering algorithms and effects.

- Optimizing rendering performance for specific hardware configurations.

- Achieving maximum utilization of GPU resources.

- Experimenting with cutting-edge rendering techniques.

While low-level GPU programming offers tremendous control and potential for optimization, it should be approached with careful consideration of its complexity and the specific needs of your graphics application. Balancing the advantages and challenges of low-level programming is essential for achieving the desired results in terms of performance and visual quality.

Section 9.5: Future of Graphics Hardware

THE FIELD OF GRAPHICS hardware is continually evolving, driven by advancements in technology, the demand for higher fidelity graphics, and the needs of various industries, including gaming, entertainment, simulation, and design. In this section, we will explore some of the emerging trends and technologies that are shaping the future of graphics hardware.

Ray Tracing Acceleration:

RAY TRACING HAS REVOLUTIONIZED computer graphics by enabling realistic rendering techniques such as global illumination, reflections, and shadows. Graphics hardware manufacturers are increasingly integrating dedicated ray tracing cores into their GPUs, making real-time ray tracing more accessible and efficient. This trend is expected to continue, leading to even more immersive and visually stunning graphics in games and applications.

AI and Machine Learning Integration:

AI AND MACHINE LEARNING are playing an increasingly significant role in graphics rendering. GPUs are being used to accelerate AI-based algorithms for tasks like denoising, upscaling, and character animation. As AI models become more sophisticated, we can expect GPUs to feature dedicated hardware for AI workloads, further enhancing graphics quality and performance.

Quantum Computing Impact:

QUANTUM COMPUTING HAS the potential to revolutionize graphics and simulation. While quantum GPUs are still in the early stages of development, they hold promise for solving complex rendering and physics simulations that are currently computationally expensive or infeasible. The integration of quantum computing into graphics hardware could lead to breakthroughs in graphics realism and simulation accuracy.

Real-time Hardware-accelerated Physics:

REALISTIC PHYSICS SIMULATIONS have always been a challenge for graphics hardware. However, with advancements in physics engines and dedicated hardware for physics calculations, future GPUs may provide real-time, highly detailed simulations of physical phenomena such as fluid dynamics, soft-body deformation, and advanced collision detection.

Customizable Graphics Pipelines:

GRAPHICS HARDWARE VENDORS are exploring ways to make the graphics pipeline more customizable by developers. This could allow game developers and content creators to define their rendering stages and shaders in more detail, tailoring the graphics pipeline to their specific needs. Customizable pipelines could lead to more diverse and innovative rendering techniques.

Increased Integration of Graphics and Compute:

THE BOUNDARY BETWEEN graphics and general-purpose computing is becoming increasingly blurred. Graphics hardware is evolving to handle a broader range of tasks beyond rendering, including AI, physics simulations, and data processing. This trend will likely result in more versatile GPUs capable of accelerating a wide variety of applications.

Energy Efficiency and Sustainability:

AS ENERGY EFFICIENCY and environmental concerns become more critical, graphics hardware manufacturers are focusing on optimizing power consumption. Future GPUs may incorporate advanced power management techniques, such as dynamic voltage and frequency scaling, to minimize energy usage while maintaining high performance.

In conclusion, the future of graphics hardware holds exciting possibilities for more realistic, efficient, and versatile graphics rendering. Ray tracing, AI integration, quantum computing, physics simulations, customizable pipelines, and energy efficiency are key areas where we can expect significant advancements. Keeping an eye on these trends and technologies is crucial for graphics developers and enthusiasts alike, as they will shape the landscape of graphics programming in the years to come.

Chapter 10: Immersive Audio Techniques

Section 10.1: Binaural and 3D Audio

In the world of graphics programming and immersive experiences, audio is a critical component that enhances realism and immersion. Binaural and 3D audio techniques play a pivotal role in creating spatial audio environments, allowing users to perceive sounds as they do in the real world. In this section, we'll delve into the concepts of binaural and 3D audio, exploring how they work, their applications, and how to implement them in your graphics projects.

Understanding Binaural Audio:

BINAURAL AUDIO IS AN audio rendering technique that mimics the way humans hear sounds in three dimensions. It relies on the principle that our ears perceive sounds differently due to their positions on either side of our head. Binaural audio takes advantage of this by processing sounds in a way that simulates how they arrive at each ear, creating a realistic sense of direction and distance.

How Binaural Audio Works:

BINAURAL AUDIO TYPICALLY involves the following key elements:

1. **Head-related transfer functions (HRTFs):** These are mathematical representations of how sounds are filtered by

the human head and ears. HRTFs are used to transform audio sources in real-time, adjusting them based on the listener's orientation, head position, and ear shape.

2. **Individualized HRTFs:** For the most convincing binaural experience, individualized HRTFs can be obtained through measurements of a person's ear shape and size. However, generic HRTFs are often used when personalization is not feasible.

3. **Stereo headphones:** Binaural audio is best experienced using high-quality stereo headphones. The precise timing and frequency adjustments applied to the audio are crucial for creating the illusion of 3D sound.

Applications of Binaural Audio:

BINAURAL AUDIO HAS a wide range of applications, including:

- **Virtual Reality (VR):** Binaural audio is essential for creating immersive VR experiences where spatial audio cues enhance realism and immersion.

- **Gaming:** Games can use binaural audio to provide players with a sense of direction and distance for in-game sounds, improving gameplay and immersion.

- **Architectural and Industrial Design:** Binaural audio can be employed to simulate the acoustic properties of spaces, aiding architects and designers in creating realistic virtual environments.

3D Audio Spatialization:

3D AUDIO GOES BEYOND binaural audio by introducing spatialization techniques that allow sound sources to be placed in three-dimensional space. This means that audio objects can have positions, orientations, and movements, just like visual objects in a 3D graphics environment.

Techniques for 3D Audio:

- **Positional Audio:** This technique involves placing sound sources at specific 3D coordinates within a virtual environment. It is commonly used in games and VR to create the illusion of sound sources moving in 3D space.

- **Ambisonics:** Ambisonics is a technique for capturing and reproducing 3D sound fields. It is often used in VR and 360-degree video to provide a sense of audio directionality.

- **Sound Propagation:** Realistic sound propagation models simulate how sound waves interact with the environment, including reflections, occlusion, and diffraction. These models contribute to the immersive quality of 3D audio.

Implementing Binaural and 3D Audio:

IMPLEMENTING BINAURAL and 3D audio in graphics projects often involves using audio middleware libraries and APIs. Some popular choices include:

- **OpenAL:** An open-source cross-platform audio API that supports 3D audio and binaural rendering.

- **FMOD Studio:** A commercial audio middleware solution that provides tools for implementing spatial audio and interactive sound design.

- **Unity 3D Audio:** If you're using Unity for game development, it offers built-in support for spatial audio and binaural rendering.

In addition to middleware, modern game engines and audio software development kits (SDKs) provide features and plugins for handling binaural and 3D audio. Integration with your graphics application allows you to synchronize visual and auditory cues, enhancing the overall immersive experience.

In conclusion, binaural and 3D audio techniques are powerful tools for enhancing the immersion and realism of graphics projects, particularly in the realms of virtual reality, gaming, and architectural visualization. Understanding how these techniques work and leveraging the appropriate audio middleware and APIs is crucial for delivering compelling and immersive audiovisual experiences.

Section 10.2: Real-time Reverberation Techniques

REAL-TIME REVERBERATION techniques are essential for creating lifelike and immersive audio environments in graphics applications, particularly in gaming, virtual reality, and architectural visualization. Reverberation, often referred to as reverb, is the persistence of sound in an environment after the original sound source has stopped emitting sound. It adds depth and realism to audio by simulating the way sound waves interact with surfaces and objects in a physical space. In this section, we'll explore the concepts of real-time reverberation and techniques to implement it in graphics projects.

Understanding Reverberation:

REVERBERATION OCCURS when sound waves bounce off surfaces, walls, and objects in an environment, creating a complex soundscape. It is an essential component of spatial audio, as it provides important cues about the size and nature of a virtual space.

How Reverberation Works:

- **Early Reflections:** When a sound is emitted, it reaches the listener's ears through two paths: direct sound and early reflections. Early reflections are the first sound waves that bounce off nearby surfaces before blending into the overall reverb.

- **Late Reverberation:** After early reflections, sound continues to reflect off surfaces multiple times, creating a diffuse and sustained reverb that characterizes the acoustic properties of the space.

Techniques for Real-time Reverberation:

IMPLEMENTING REAL-TIME reverberation involves using algorithms and techniques to simulate the complex behavior of sound in virtual environments. Here are some common techniques:

1. Convolution Reverb:

CONVOLUTION REVERB is a widely used technique that simulates reverb by convolving the audio signal with an impulse response (IR) recorded from a real-world location. The IR represents how sound bounces off surfaces in that space. Convolution reverb is computationally intensive but provides highly realistic results.

// Pseudo code for convolution reverb

output = Convolve(audio_input, impulse_response);

2. Parametric Reverb Models:

PARAMETRIC MODELS USE mathematical equations to simulate reverb based on the characteristics of the virtual space. They offer real-time performance but may lack the nuanced realism of convolution reverb.

// Pseudo code for parametric reverb

output = ParametricReverb(audio_input, room_size, absorption_coefficient);

3. Feedback Delay Networks (FDN):

FDN IS A RECURSIVE algorithm that models reverb as feedback delay lines. It's efficient and suitable for real-time applications. FDNs can simulate a wide range of reverb characteristics, from small rooms to vast cathedrals.

// Pseudo code for FDN reverb

output = FeedbackDelayNetworkReverb(audio_input, room_size, reflection_count);

Integration with Graphics:

TO ACHIEVE A SEAMLESS audio-visual experience, real-time reverberation must be synchronized with the visual elements of a graphics application. This involves matching the audio cues with the virtual environment's geometry, ensuring that sound reflects off surfaces in a physically plausible manner.

In game engines like Unity and Unreal Engine, audio and graphics systems are integrated, allowing developers to place audio emitters and receivers in the scene. Audio occlusion and obstruction, where objects block sound propagation, are also considered to enhance realism.

Conclusion:

REAL-TIME REVERBERATION is a crucial component of immersive audio in graphics projects. By simulating the way sound interacts with virtual environments, it adds depth and authenticity to the overall experience. Whether using convolution reverb, parametric models, or feedback delay networks, understanding and implementing reverberation techniques can greatly enhance the audio quality and immersion of your graphics applications.

Section 10.3: Advanced Audio Simulation

ADVANCED AUDIO SIMULATION techniques are essential for creating rich and immersive audio experiences in graphics applications. These techniques go beyond basic sound playback and involve the modeling of complex audio behaviors, such as sound propagation, reflection, occlusion, and dynamic environmental effects. In this section, we'll delve into the concepts and methods behind advanced audio simulation in graphics.

Modeling Sound Propagation:

IN THE REAL WORLD, sound doesn't simply emanate from a source and reach the listener. It interacts with the environment, reflecting off surfaces, diffracting around obstacles, and being absorbed by materials. To achieve realism, graphics applications must simulate these behaviors.

Ray Tracing for Audio:

ONE APPROACH TO SOUND propagation modeling is using ray tracing techniques similar to those employed in rendering graphics. Sound rays are cast from the source, and their interactions with the environment are calculated. This can result in accurate sound propagation, including reflections and occlusion.

```
// Pseudo code for ray tracing-based sound propagation

for each sound ray {

trace_ray_through_environment(ray);

apply_reflection_and_occlusion_effects(ray);

calculate_sound_attenuation(ray);

accumulate_sound_energy_at_listener(ray);

}
```

Dynamic Environmental Effects:

IN DYNAMIC ENVIRONMENTS, audio simulation must account for changes such as moving objects, changing materials, and variable room configurations. These changes can affect sound propagation and perception.

Real-time Environmental Changes:

GRAPHICS APPLICATIONS should dynamically update audio simulations based on changes in the environment. For example, if a character moves from an open field into a cave, the audio simulation should adapt to the new acoustic properties of the cave.

// Pseudo code for real-time environmental changes

```
if character_enters_cave {

update_environment_acoustics(cave_properties);

}
```

Ambisonics and Spatial Audio:

AMBISONICS IS A TECHNIQUE used to represent and render three-dimensional sound fields. It's particularly valuable for VR and AR applications where the listener's head orientation changes. Spatial audio systems employ techniques like Ambisonics to provide a realistic sense of sound direction and location.

// Pseudo code for Ambisonics sound rendering

```
initialize_ambisonics_renderer();

set_listener_orientation(listener_orientation);
```

render_spatial_audio(source_positions);

Integration with Graphics:

TO ACHIEVE A SEAMLESS audio-visual experience, advanced audio simulation techniques must be tightly integrated with the graphics rendering pipeline. This integration ensures that audio reflects the visual elements accurately.

Game engines and graphics frameworks often provide tools for this integration, allowing developers to place audio emitters and receivers within the 3D scene. Audio occlusion, where objects block sound propagation, is also considered to enhance realism.

Conclusion:

ADVANCED AUDIO SIMULATION techniques play a critical role in creating immersive graphics applications. By modeling sound propagation, accounting for dynamic environmental changes, and employing spatial audio techniques like Ambisonics, developers can create audio experiences that enhance realism and immersion. Integrating these techniques with the graphics rendering pipeline ensures that the audio and visual elements of an application are in harmony, delivering a compelling and believable user experience.

Section 10.4: Sound Propagation in Complex Environments

SOUND PROPAGATION IN complex environments presents a unique challenge in graphics applications. Unlike simple scenes with a single sound source and listener, complex environments involve multiple sound sources, reflective surfaces, and occluding objects. In this section, we will explore techniques and considerations for simulating sound propagation in such scenarios.

Reflection and Reverberation:

IN A COMPLEX ENVIRONMENT, sound waves interact with various surfaces, leading to reflections and reverberation. These phenomena significantly impact the perception of the audio's spatial characteristics and contribute to the overall realism of the scene.

Ray-Tracing-Based Reflection:

TO SIMULATE SOUND REFLECTION, ray-tracing techniques can be employed. Rays are cast from the sound source, and their paths are traced to determine which surfaces they interact with. When a ray hits a surface, it generates a reflected sound wave that contributes to the overall sound.

```
// Pseudo code for ray-tracing-based sound reflection

for each sound ray {

trace_ray_to_surface(ray);

if (ray_hits_surface) {

generate_reflected_sound_wave(ray, surface_properties);

}

}
```

Reverberation Modeling:

REVERBERATION IS THE persistence of sound in an environment due to multiple reflections. It can be simulated using techniques like convolution reverb, where impulse responses for different surfaces and materials are convolved with the sound signal.

```
// Pseudo code for convolution reverb

for each sound source {

calculate_impulse_response(sound_source_position,
environment_properties);

convolve_sound_signal_with_impulse_response(sound_signal,
impulse_response);

}
```

Occlusion and Diffraction:

IN COMPLEX ENVIRONMENTS, sound can be obstructed or diffracted around objects. This adds to the complexity of sound propagation modeling.

Occlusion Effects:

OCCLUSION OCCURS WHEN sound waves are blocked by objects, resulting in a muffled or attenuated sound. To simulate occlusion, the application must determine which objects obstruct the sound path and calculate the degree of attenuation.

```
// Pseudo code for sound occlusion

for each sound ray {

check_for_occluding_objects(ray);

if (occlusion_detected) {

calculate_occlusion_attenuation(ray, occluding_object_properties);

}
```

}

Diffraction:

WHEN SOUND ENCOUNTERS obstacles, it can diffract around them, leading to the phenomenon known as diffraction. Modeling diffraction requires considering the wavelength of sound and the geometry of obstacles.

Real-Time Updates:

COMPLEX ENVIRONMENTS may undergo dynamic changes, such as the movement of objects or alterations in room configurations. Real-time updates to the sound simulation are essential to maintain realism.

// Pseudo code for real-time environment updates

if object_moves {

update_sound_simulation(object_new_position);

}

Integration with Graphics:

TO PROVIDE A SEAMLESS audio-visual experience, sound propagation in complex environments should be tightly integrated with the graphics rendering pipeline. This integration ensures that audio reflects the visual elements accurately.

In conclusion, simulating sound propagation in complex environments is crucial for creating immersive graphics applications. Techniques like ray-tracing-based reflection, convolution reverb, and occlusion modeling enhance the realism of audio experiences.

Dynamic updates and integration with the graphics rendering pipeline ensure that sound and visuals are synchronized, contributing to a compelling user experience.

Section 10.5: Audio Shaders and Processing

AUDIO SHADERS AND PROCESSING play a vital role in modern graphics applications, enriching the audio experience and enhancing immersion. In this section, we delve into the world of audio shaders, real-time audio processing, and their integration with graphics.

Audio Shaders:

AUDIO SHADERS ARE ANALOGOUS to graphics shaders but are designed to manipulate audio data. They allow developers to create real-time audio effects, such as filtering, modulation, and spatialization. These audio shaders are executed on the GPU or specialized audio processing units, enabling high-performance audio processing.

```
// Example HLSL audio shader for reverb effect

float3    AudioShaderReverb(float3    audioSample,    float3 reverbParameters) {

// Apply reverb effect to audio sample

// ...

return processedAudioSample;

}
```

Real-time Audio Processing:

REAL-TIME AUDIO PROCESSING involves applying various effects and transformations to audio data in real-time. This is commonly used for effects like equalization, delay, and spatial audio positioning. The processing can be performed on the GPU or dedicated audio hardware.

```cpp
// Example C++ code for real-time audio processing

void RealTimeAudioProcessing(AudioBuffer& input, AudioBuffer& output, AudioEffectParameters& parameters) {

// Apply audio effects to input buffer and store the result in the output buffer

// ...

}
```

Integration with Graphics:

INTEGRATING AUDIO SHADERS and real-time audio processing with graphics is essential for creating immersive multimedia experiences. This integration ensures that audio effects respond to changes in the visual environment, enhancing the overall coherence of the application.

```cpp
// Example C++ code for synchronizing audio and graphics

void UpdateAudioEffects(GraphicsScene& scene, AudioEngine& audio) {

// Extract relevant data from the graphics scene

AudioEffectParameters audioParameters = ExtractAudioParameters(scene);
```

```
// Apply audio effects using real-time processing

RealTimeAudioProcessing(audioParameters);

// Update the audio engine with the processed audio

audio.UpdateAudioOutput(audioParameters);

}
```

Spatial Audio:

SPATIAL AUDIO TECHNIQUES enable the positioning of audio sources in 3D space, providing a more immersive experience. This involves simulating how sound waves propagate and interact with the environment, giving users a sense of audio depth and direction.

```
// Example C# code for spatial audio in a game engine

void UpdateAudioPosition(Vector3 listenerPosition, Vector3 soundSourcePosition) {

// Calculate the audio spatialization parameters based on listener and source positions

AudioSpatializationParameters spatializationParameters = CalculateSpatializationParameters(listenerPosition, soundSourcePosition);

// Apply spatialization to the audio source

ApplySpatialization(audioSource, spatializationParameters);

}
```

Dynamic Audio Environments:

MODERN GRAPHICS APPLICATIONS often feature dynamic environments where objects move, and scenes change. Audio shaders and real-time audio processing should adapt to these dynamic changes to maintain synchronization between audio and graphics.

```
// Example HLSL code for dynamic audio shader adaptation

float3    DynamicAudioShader(float3    audioSample,    float3
dynamicParameters) {

// Adjust audio processing based on dynamic changes

// ...

return processedAudioSample;

}
```

In conclusion, audio shaders and real-time audio processing are crucial components of contemporary graphics applications. They enable developers to create immersive audio experiences that complement the visual elements. Integration with graphics, spatial audio techniques, and adaptability to dynamic environments ensure that audio enhances the overall user experience, making multimedia applications more engaging and realistic.

Chapter 11: Procedural Generation Techniques

Section 11.1: Procedural Modelling and Texturing

Procedural generation is a powerful technique used in computer graphics and game development to create content algorithmically rather than manually. In this section, we'll explore procedural modeling and texturing, which are fundamental aspects of procedural content generation.

Procedural modeling involves generating 3D models and scenes using algorithms. Instead of designing models vertex by vertex, procedural modeling techniques use mathematical rules to define shapes, structures, and details. This approach is particularly useful for generating terrain, buildings, vegetation, and other complex environments in games and simulations.

One common procedural modeling technique is fractal-based terrain generation. Fractals are mathematical constructs that exhibit self-similarity at different scales. When applied to terrain, fractals can create natural-looking landscapes with features such as mountains, valleys, and rivers. Algorithms like the Diamond-Square algorithm and Perlin noise are commonly used for terrain generation.

In addition to terrain, procedural modeling can be applied to architecture and city generation. Algorithms can define building shapes, street layouts, and even interior designs. This is especially valuable for open-world games where vast urban environments need to be created efficiently.

Procedural texturing, on the other hand, involves generating textures algorithmically. This technique is used to create detailed and diverse textures for surfaces in a virtual environment. Procedural textures are not limited by resolution, and they can adapt to the scale of the object they're applied to, ensuring consistent quality.

One popular approach to procedural texturing is the use of shader programs, such as those in OpenGL or Vulkan. These shaders define how textures are generated based on mathematical functions and noise patterns. By adjusting parameters and combining different noise functions, developers can create textures that simulate materials like marble, wood, or even complex patterns like camouflage.

Procedural generation is not limited to a single domain. It can be combined with other techniques, such as physics simulations, to create dynamic and interactive content. For example, procedural modeling can be used to generate trees and vegetation, while procedural texturing can define the appearance of their leaves and bark. When integrated with a physics engine, these trees can respond realistically to wind and collisions.

In conclusion, procedural modeling and texturing are powerful tools for creating content in computer graphics and games. They enable developers to generate complex and diverse environments and textures algorithmically, reducing the need for manual asset creation. When used creatively, procedural generation can result in dynamic, interactive, and visually stunning virtual worlds. Throughout this chapter, we'll delve deeper into various procedural generation techniques and their applications in graphics and game development.

```glsl
// Example procedural texture generation shader in OpenGL

#version 330 core

out vec4 FragColor;

void main()

{

// Generate a checkerboard pattern

vec2 uv = gl_FragCoord.xy / vec2(800, 600);

int checker = int(mod(floor(uv.x * 8.0) + floor(uv.y * 8.0), 2.0));

FragColor = vec4(vec3(checker), 1.0);

}
```

In the code snippet above, we generate a simple checkerboard pattern using a fragment shader in OpenGL. This demonstrates the basic concept of procedural texturing, where the texture color is calculated algorithmically based on the UV coordinates of the fragment.

Throughout this chapter, we'll explore more advanced procedural modeling and texturing techniques and how they can be applied to various aspects of graphics and game development.

Section 11.2: Infinite Worlds and Fractal Geometry

INFINITE WORLDS ARE a fascinating concept in game development and computer graphics. They offer players vast, procedurally generated environments to explore without the limitations of finite maps. Achieving infinite worlds often involves the use of fractal geometry and procedural techniques. In this section, we'll delve into the principles of creating infinite worlds through fractal geometry.

Fractal geometry plays a fundamental role in generating complex, self-similar structures that can be scaled indefinitely. Fractals are mathematical shapes that exhibit intricate detail at all levels of magnification. They are particularly well-suited for creating terrain, landscapes, and structures that appear natural and organic.

One of the most famous fractal-based algorithms used in terrain generation is the Diamond-Square algorithm. This algorithm starts with a square grid and recursively subdivides it into smaller squares and diamonds. At each iteration, the algorithm calculates the midpoint between the vertices of squares and diamonds and adds a random displacement. This process is repeated, creating a terrain with realistic features like mountains and valleys.

Another widely used technique is Perlin noise, which generates smooth, continuous noise patterns. It's often used to add variation to terrain and textures. Perlin noise can be applied in multiple dimensions and can create intricate, natural-looking patterns, making it a valuable tool for creating terrain, clouds, and other natural phenomena.

Infinite worlds are not limited to terrain generation. They can also include procedural cityscapes, caves, and dungeons. The key to achieving infinite worlds is to generate content on the fly as the player explores the environment. This is commonly done using a combination of procedural generation algorithms and spatial partitioning techniques to efficiently load and render only the portions of the world that are visible to the player.

For example, in a game with an infinite procedurally generated terrain, the terrain chunks that are far from the player's current position may not need to be loaded or rendered until the player approaches them. This ensures efficient use of memory and processing power.

Infinite worlds are not without challenges. Managing memory, ensuring seamless transitions between chunks, and maintaining consistency in the generated content are all important considerations. Additionally, the procedural algorithms used should be designed to allow for smooth transitions and coherent overall world design.

 # Python pseudocode for generating an infinite fractal terrain using the Diamond-Square algorithm

```python
def generate_infinite_terrain(size, roughness):

    terrain = initialize_terrain(size)

    step_size = size - 1

    while step_size > 1:

        diamond_step(terrain, step_size, roughness)

        square_step(terrain, step_size, roughness)

        step_size //= 2

        roughness *= 0.5

    return terrain
```

The pseudocode above outlines a simplified version of the Diamond-Square algorithm for generating an infinite fractal terrain. This algorithm is iteratively applied, reducing the step size and adjusting the roughness parameter for each iteration, resulting in increasingly detailed terrain.

Infinite worlds and fractal geometry open up exciting possibilities for game developers and artists. They allow for the creation of expansive, diverse, and visually captivating virtual worlds that players can explore endlessly. By harnessing the power of procedural generation and fractals, developers can craft unique and immersive gaming experiences that feel boundless in scale and detail.

Section 11.3: Real-time Ray Tracing

REAL-TIME RAY TRACING is a groundbreaking rendering technique that has revolutionized computer graphics by enabling highly realistic lighting and reflections. Traditionally, rasterization has been the standard method for rendering in real-time graphics, but ray tracing offers a more physically accurate approach. In this section, we'll explore the fundamentals of real-time ray tracing and its applications in modern graphics.

Ray tracing simulates the behavior of light rays as they interact with objects in a scene. Unlike rasterization, which projects 3D objects onto a 2D screen, ray tracing works by tracing rays of light as they travel from the camera through each pixel on the screen and into the scene. This process allows for the accurate simulation of effects like shadows, reflections, refractions, and global illumination.

The core concept of ray tracing is the "ray-object intersection." For each pixel on the screen, a primary ray is cast from the camera's position, and its path is traced until it intersects with an object in the scene. When an intersection occurs, the renderer can calculate various lighting effects at that point, such as diffuse and specular reflections.

One of the primary advantages of real-time ray tracing is its ability to handle complex lighting scenarios effortlessly. It accurately models the way light interacts with materials, allowing for realistic effects like soft shadows, ambient occlusion, and global illumination. This results in scenes that look closer to real-life photography.

The introduction of hardware-accelerated ray tracing, such as NVIDIA's RTX series and AMD's RDNA2 architecture, has made real-time ray tracing practical for gaming. These GPUs include specialized hardware to accelerate ray tracing calculations, making it possible to achieve high frame rates while maintaining stunning visual fidelity.

In addition to primary rays, real-time ray tracing also involves secondary rays. Secondary rays are generated when a primary ray intersects with a reflective or refractive surface. These secondary rays can simulate effects like reflections and refractions accurately.

```cpp
// C++ pseudocode for casting primary and secondary rays in real-time ray tracing

Color castPrimaryRay(const Ray& primaryRay, const Scene& scene) {

Intersection intersection;

if (scene.intersect(primaryRay, intersection)) {

// Calculate lighting at the intersection point

// ...

// Cast secondary rays for reflections and refractions

Color reflection = castReflectionRay(primaryRay, intersection, scene);
```

```
Color refraction = castRefractionRay(primaryRay, intersection,
scene);
```

```
// Combine primary, reflection, and refraction colors
```

```
Color finalColor = calculateFinalColor(primaryColor, reflection,
refraction);
```

```
return finalColor;
```

```
}
```

```
return backgroundColor;
```

```
}
```

In the pseudocode above, we see the process of casting primary and secondary rays in a real-time ray tracing renderer. Primary rays are cast from the camera, and secondary rays are generated when needed to simulate reflections and refractions.

Real-time ray tracing has brought a new level of realism and immersion to video games and other interactive applications. As hardware continues to advance, we can expect even more impressive ray tracing effects and increasingly photorealistic virtual worlds in the future.

Section 11.4: Subsurface Scattering Implementation

SUBSURFACE SCATTERING (SSS) is a rendering technique used to simulate the behavior of light as it penetrates and scatters within translucent materials such as skin, wax, and milk. It's a crucial aspect of rendering realistic characters and objects in computer graphics, as it adds depth and believability to the appearance of these materials. In this section, we'll delve into the implementation of subsurface scattering in real-time rendering.

The Physics of Subsurface Scattering

BEFORE WE DIVE INTO the implementation details, it's essential to understand the physical basis of subsurface scattering. When light enters a translucent material, it can scatter in multiple directions rather than following a direct path. The extent and pattern of this scattering depend on various factors, including the material's thickness, composition, and the incident angle of light.

One of the most common models used for simulating subsurface scattering is the diffusion approximation. This model treats the material as a participating medium, where light is absorbed and re-emitted multiple times within the material. The result is that light appears to penetrate and scatter beneath the surface, creating a soft and realistic appearance.

Implementation Steps

IMPLEMENTING SUBSURFACE scattering in real-time rendering involves several key steps:

1. **Light Transport Simulation**: The first step is to simulate the transport of light within the material. This is typically done using a numerical technique such as Monte Carlo ray tracing. Rays of light are traced as they enter the material, scatter, and exit. At each scattering event, the ray's energy is attenuated based on the material's absorption and scattering coefficients.

2. **BSSRDF Calculation**: The Bidirectional Surface Scattering Reflectance Distribution Function (BSSRDF) describes how light scatters within the material. It's a

critical component of subsurface scattering. The BSSRDF is calculated based on the material's properties and is used to model the diffusion of light.

3. **Integration over All Incident Directions**: To compute the final appearance of a point on the surface, you need to integrate the scattered light arriving from all incident directions. This involves sampling incoming light directions and evaluating the BSSRDF at each point.

4. **Efficient Approximations**: Real-time implementations often rely on approximations to reduce the computational complexity. Techniques like screen-space subsurface scattering and precomputed diffusion profiles are used to speed up rendering while maintaining visual fidelity.

Here's a simplified example of how subsurface scattering might be implemented in a shader:

```hlsl
// HLSL pseudocode for subsurface scattering shader

float3 SubsurfaceScattering(float3 surfaceColor, float3 normal, float3 viewDir, float3 lightDir)

{

// Calculate the BSSRDF based on material properties

float3 bssrdf = ComputeBSSRDF(normal, viewDir, lightDir);

// Approximate the subsurface scattering effect

float3 sssColor = surfaceColor * bssrdf;

return sssColor;

}
```

In this HLSL pseudocode, we calculate the subsurface scattering effect by evaluating the BSSRDF and applying it to the surface color. Real implementations would involve more complex calculations and optimizations.

Subsurface scattering is a computationally intensive technique, and achieving real-time performance requires clever approximations and optimizations. Nevertheless, when implemented correctly, it significantly enhances the realism of rendered characters and materials.

Section 11.5: Dynamic Story and World Generation

DYNAMIC STORY AND WORLD generation is a fascinating aspect of game development that allows for the creation of ever-evolving game worlds and narratives. This approach can enhance player engagement by offering unique experiences in each playthrough. In this section, we'll explore the concepts and techniques behind dynamic story and world generation in games.

The Concept of Dynamic Generation

DYNAMIC STORY AND WORLD generation involves creating game content on-the-fly or procedurally. Instead of pre-designing every aspect of the game world, developers employ algorithms and systems to generate various elements such as landscapes, characters, quests, and narratives in response to player actions, choices, or randomization. This dynamic approach can lead to non-linear gameplay experiences and replayability.

Techniques for Dynamic World Generation

Procedural Generation:

PROCEDURAL GENERATION is a core technique for dynamic world generation. It involves using algorithms to generate content algorithmically rather than manually designing it. This can apply to terrain generation, level design, and even the creation of NPCs and items. Procedural generation algorithms are often used to create vast and diverse game worlds.

Randomization:

RANDOMIZATION IS A simpler form of dynamic generation. It involves introducing randomness or uncertainty into various aspects of the game. For example, loot drops, enemy spawns, or weather conditions can be randomized to make each playthrough unique.

Decision Trees:

DECISION TREES ARE used to create branching narratives in games. They allow for player choices to influence the outcome of the story. The choices players make at various points in the game can lead to different narrative paths, creating a dynamic and interactive storytelling experience.

Simulation:

SIMULATION-BASED DYNAMIC generation involves modeling complex systems within the game world. For instance, a city-building game might simulate the growth and interactions of virtual citizens, leading to emergent gameplay scenarios. Simulations can result in dynamic and unpredictable game worlds.

Challenges and Considerations

WHILE DYNAMIC GENERATION offers exciting possibilities, it also presents challenges:

Balancing:

BALANCING A DYNAMICALLY generated game world can be complex. Developers must ensure that generated content remains challenging and enjoyable for players, even as it changes.

Player Agency:

DYNAMIC GENERATION can be a double-edged sword regarding player agency. While it empowers players to shape the game world, it can also make it difficult to craft meaningful stories and experiences.

Content Quality:

PROCEDURALLY GENERATED or dynamically generated content may lack the quality and craftsmanship of hand-designed elements. Striking a balance between quantity and quality is crucial.

Technical Complexity:

IMPLEMENTING DYNAMIC generation systems requires a deep understanding of algorithms, data structures, and game design principles. It can be technically challenging to create seamless and engaging dynamic experiences.

Examples of Dynamic Generation

SEVERAL GAMES HAVE successfully implemented dynamic story and world generation:

- **Roguelikes**: Games like "The Binding of Isaac" and "Spelunky" use procedural generation to create unique levels and challenges in each playthrough.

- **RPGs**: Titles like "The Elder Scrolls" series employ procedural generation for terrain and quests, offering vast open worlds with endless possibilities.

- **Narrative-driven Games**: "Detroit: Become Human" and "Until Dawn" use decision trees and player choices to create branching narratives.

Dynamic story and world generation can add depth, variety, and replayability to games, making it an exciting field for game developers to explore. However, it also demands careful design and technical expertise to deliver compelling and coherent experiences to players.

Chapter 12: Mixed Reality Rendering

Section 12.1: Merging VR and AR Techniques

Mixed Reality (MR) is an exciting frontier in the realm of immersive experiences, where virtual and augmented realities converge to create new interactive possibilities. This section delves into the merging of Virtual Reality (VR) and Augmented Reality (AR) techniques to provide users with compelling mixed reality experiences.

Understanding Mixed Reality

MIXED REALITY SITS on a spectrum between the fully immersive Virtual Reality (VR) and the augmentation of the real world with Augmented Reality (AR). In MR, digital content seamlessly interacts with the physical environment, allowing users to engage with virtual objects as if they coexist with the real world. Achieving this illusion requires a blend of advanced rendering techniques, tracking, and user interaction methods.

Combining VR and AR Technologies

TO CREATE MR EXPERIENCES, developers leverage the technologies from both VR and AR:

1. Tracking Systems:

- **Inside-out Tracking**: This technique enables devices to track their position and orientation in the physical space.

Cameras and sensors on the MR headset or handheld devices scan the surroundings and recognize physical objects, allowing the system to place virtual objects accurately within the real world.

2. Rendering:

- **Depth Sensing**: MR devices often incorporate depth-sensing cameras or LIDAR to capture the 3D structure of the environment. This depth data is crucial for occlusion, spatial mapping, and realistic object placement.

- **Real-time Occlusion**: To make virtual objects appear as if they interact with real-world objects, real-time occlusion rendering techniques are employed. Virtual objects are occluded by real objects in the user's view, creating a convincing mixed reality scene.

3. Interaction:

- **Gesture Recognition**: Gesture recognition technology enables users to interact with virtual objects using hand gestures. Cameras and sensors track hand movements, allowing users to manipulate and control the digital content.

- **Haptic Feedback**: Haptic feedback devices provide tactile sensations to users when they interact with virtual objects, enhancing the sense of presence in the mixed reality environment.

Applications of MR

MIXED REALITY HAS A wide range of applications, including:

- **Gaming**: MR gaming experiences enable users to play in their physical surroundings while interacting with virtual game elements.

- **Education**: MR can revolutionize education by offering immersive learning experiences, such as exploring historical events or dissecting virtual biology specimens.

- **Architecture and Design**: Architects and designers use MR to visualize and interact with 3D models of buildings and products.

- **Training and Simulation**: MR is valuable for training simulations in various industries, from healthcare to aviation.

- **Collaboration**: Remote collaboration becomes more engaging with MR, where users from different locations can interact in a shared virtual space.

Challenges and Future Trends

WHILE MR HOLDS IMMENSE promise, it faces several challenges:

- **Hardware Limitations**: Achieving seamless MR experiences requires advanced hardware, which may be expensive and inaccessible to many users.

- **Content Creation**: Creating high-quality MR content demands specialized skills and tools.

- **Privacy and Security**: MR raises concerns about data privacy and security, especially when depth-sensing cameras are used to capture the physical environment.

The future of mixed reality holds exciting possibilities. As hardware becomes more accessible and content creation tools improve, MR is poised to revolutionize how we interact with digital information and the physical world, offering new dimensions of immersion and interactivity.

Section 12.2: Real-time Object Tracking

REAL-TIME OBJECT TRACKING is a fundamental component of mixed reality (MR) systems, enabling the accurate positioning and interaction of virtual objects within the user's physical environment. In this section, we explore the techniques and technologies behind real-time object tracking in the context of MR.

Tracking Technologies

1. Visual SLAM (Simultaneous Localization and Mapping)

- Visual SLAM is a key technology for MR. It uses cameras to simultaneously map the physical environment and track the user's device within that environment.

- The device's camera captures images of the surroundings, and algorithms analyze these images to identify and track feature points, such as corners or edges. By comparing feature points between frames, the device can estimate its position and orientation in real-time.

• Visual SLAM is commonly used in handheld MR devices like smartphones and tablets. It allows users to place virtual objects on surfaces or move around them.

2. LIDAR (Light Detection and Ranging)

• LIDAR is a remote sensing method that uses laser light to measure distances to objects. In MR, LIDAR sensors are often used for accurate depth sensing.

• LIDAR sensors emit laser pulses and measure the time it takes for the light to bounce back. This information is used to create detailed 3D maps of the environment.

• LIDAR provides highly accurate depth data, enabling precise object placement and occlusion in MR experiences. It is commonly found in high-end MR headsets.

3. Inertial Sensors

• Inertial sensors, including accelerometers and gyroscopes, are used to measure the device's motion and orientation.

• These sensors provide short-term tracking data and help correct drift in long-term tracking methods like Visual SLAM.

• Inertial sensors are crucial for maintaining accurate tracking when visual tracking methods may lose track of the environment.

Challenges in Object Tracking

REAL-TIME OBJECT TRACKING in MR is not without its challenges:

- **Latency**: Achieving low-latency tracking is crucial for a smooth and immersive MR experience. Any delay in tracking data can lead to discomfort or motion sickness.

- **Environment Variability**: Real-world environments can vary greatly, from well-lit rooms to outdoor settings. MR systems need to adapt to these variations for reliable tracking.

- **Occlusion Handling**: Handling occlusion, where virtual objects are hidden behind real-world objects, is challenging. Real-time occlusion rendering techniques are necessary for a convincing MR experience.

- **Hardware Constraints**: Mobile MR devices often have limited computational power and battery life, making it challenging to implement complex tracking algorithms.

Use Cases for Object Tracking in MR

REAL-TIME OBJECT TRACKING enables a wide range of MR applications:

- **Object Placement**: Users can place virtual objects on physical surfaces or within the environment, allowing for interactive experiences.

- **Spatial Interaction**: MR applications can respond to gestures and movements within the tracked space, creating intuitive user interfaces.

- **Remote Collaboration**: MR enables multiple users to interact with virtual objects in a shared physical space, even if they are in different locations.

- **Training and Simulation**: MR can provide realistic training scenarios by overlaying virtual elements onto the real world.

Future Trends

THE FUTURE OF REAL-time object tracking in MR is promising. As hardware becomes more capable and affordable, and tracking algorithms become more sophisticated, we can expect even more immersive and interactive MR experiences. Additionally, advances in machine learning and computer vision will play a significant role in improving tracking accuracy and robustness in various lighting and environmental conditions.

Section 12.3: Scene Reconstruction from Video

SCENE RECONSTRUCTION from video is a fascinating field in mixed reality (MR) and computer vision, where the goal is to create a 3D representation of the environment using one or more video cameras. This section explores the techniques and technologies behind scene reconstruction and its applications in MR.

Techniques for Scene Reconstruction

1. Structure from Motion (SfM)

- SfM is a technique that reconstructs the 3D structure of an environment by analyzing the motion of a camera.

• It works by identifying and tracking feature points in consecutive frames of a video. By analyzing how these points move, SfM can estimate the camera's motion and the 3D positions of the tracked features.

• SfM is suitable for reconstructing static scenes and is often used in applications like 3D modeling, augmented reality, and virtual reality.

2. Depth Sensing and RGB-D Cameras

• RGB-D cameras, such as the Microsoft Kinect, provide color (RGB) and depth (D) information for each pixel in an image.

• Using depth information, it is possible to create dense 3D reconstructions of environments by aligning multiple depth frames.

• RGB-D cameras are commonly used in applications that require real-time scene reconstruction, like indoor navigation for robots and MR headset tracking.

3. Multi-View Stereo (MVS)

• MVS is a technique that combines information from multiple camera views to create detailed 3D reconstructions.

• It works by identifying common features in overlapping camera views and triangulating their 3D positions.

- MVS is often used in applications that require highly detailed reconstructions, such as archaeological site documentation and cultural heritage preservation.

Applications of Scene Reconstruction in MR

SCENE RECONSTRUCTION has several valuable applications in MR:

- **Environmental Mapping**: MR devices can use scene reconstructions for mapping and localization, allowing users to move within an environment while keeping virtual objects anchored to real-world locations.

- **Object Interaction**: Scene reconstructions enable realistic object interactions in MR. Virtual objects can collide with real-world surfaces and respond accurately to lighting conditions.

- **Realistic Avatars**: In social VR and MR experiences, scene reconstruction helps create realistic avatars by capturing the user's facial expressions and gestures.

- **Architectural Visualization**: Architects and designers can use MR with scene reconstruction to visualize architectural designs in real-world contexts.

Challenges and Future Directions

DESPITE SIGNIFICANT progress, challenges remain in scene reconstruction from video:

- **Real-time Processing**: Achieving real-time scene reconstruction on consumer-grade hardware is still a challenge. Future advancements in hardware and algorithms are necessary to overcome this.

- **Scalability**: Large-scale scene reconstructions, like city-scale mapping, are computationally intensive. Research in distributed reconstruction and efficient data storage is ongoing.

- **Dynamic Scenes**: Handling dynamic scenes with moving objects and people remains a challenge. Techniques to distinguish between static and dynamic elements need further development.

The future of scene reconstruction in MR holds promise. As technology continues to advance, we can expect more seamless and realistic mixed reality experiences. This includes better real-time reconstruction, more detailed and accurate models, and increased compatibility with various MR devices and platforms.

Section 12.4: Real-world Lighting in AR

BRINGING REALISTIC lighting into augmented reality (AR) experiences is crucial for creating convincing and immersive mixed reality environments. This section delves into the challenges and techniques involved in achieving real-world lighting in AR applications.

Challenges in Real-world Lighting

ACHIEVING REALISTIC lighting in AR involves overcoming several challenges:

1. Light Estimation:

- AR applications need to estimate the intensity, color, and direction of real-world light sources accurately.

- This estimation helps virtual objects blend seamlessly with the real environment and respond to changes in lighting conditions.

2. Consistency:

- Maintaining lighting consistency between virtual and real objects is essential. Virtual objects should cast shadows and receive reflections just like real objects.

- Achieving this consistency is complex due to variations in real-world lighting.

3. Dynamic Lighting:

- AR users move around and interact with virtual objects, making it challenging to maintain consistent lighting in dynamic scenes.

- Real-time adaptation to changes in lighting conditions is necessary for a convincing AR experience.

4. Real-time Rendering:

- AR applications must perform real-time rendering while considering the complex interactions between virtual and real-world lighting.

- This requires efficient algorithms and hardware.

Techniques for Real-world Lighting in AR

1. Light Probes:

- Light probes capture the surrounding environment's lighting information, allowing virtual objects to reflect the real-world lighting.

- These probes can be placed in the scene to sample lighting conditions and apply them to virtual objects.

2. Image-based Lighting (IBL):

- IBL techniques use high-dynamic-range (HDR) images of the real environment to illuminate virtual objects.

- These images capture the entire lighting environment, including indirect lighting and reflections.

3. Local Illumination Models:

- Local illumination models, such as Phong and Blinn-Phong, simulate the interaction between virtual objects and direct lighting sources.

- While these models are less physically accurate than global illumination, they can be used in real-time AR rendering.

4. Global Illumination:

- For more realistic results, global illumination techniques like radiosity and ray tracing can be applied to AR.

- These methods simulate the complex interplay of light in a scene but are computationally intensive.

5. Shadow Mapping:

- Shadow mapping techniques create shadows for virtual objects based on the position and intensity of real-world light sources.

- This enhances the realism of AR scenes by ensuring that virtual objects cast shadows.

Hardware Considerations

TO ACHIEVE REAL-WORLD lighting in AR, hardware plays a significant role:

- **Sensors**: High-quality light sensors are essential for accurate light estimation. Modern AR devices often include dedicated sensors for this purpose.

- **Displays**: AR headsets need displays with good color accuracy and high dynamic range to render scenes realistically.

- **Graphics Processing Unit (GPU)**: Powerful GPUs are necessary for real-time rendering with complex lighting models.

Future Directions

THE FUTURE OF REAL-world lighting in AR looks promising:

- **Improved Sensors**: Advancements in sensor technology will lead to more accurate light estimation, making virtual objects appear even more integrated into the real world.

- **Real-time Ray Tracing**: As GPUs become more capable, real-time ray tracing may become more practical in AR, further enhancing lighting realism.

- **AI-driven Lighting**: Machine learning techniques can be used to predict and simulate real-world lighting conditions, improving consistency and dynamic adaptability.

In conclusion, achieving real-world lighting in AR is a challenging but essential aspect of creating immersive mixed reality experiences. With advancements in hardware and rendering techniques, we can expect AR to become even more visually convincing in the future.

Section 12.5: Physical and Virtual Interactions

IN THE REALM OF MIXED reality (MR), interactions that seamlessly blend the physical and virtual worlds are a fundamental aspect. This section explores techniques and considerations for achieving natural and intuitive physical and virtual interactions in MR applications.

The Challenge of Interactions

CREATING COMPELLING MR experiences involves overcoming several challenges related to interactions:

1. Realism:

- To provide a truly immersive MR experience, interactions should mimic real-world behaviors and physics.

- Users should feel like their virtual actions have real consequences.

2. Precision:

- MR interactions often require precise tracking and alignment of virtual objects with the physical environment.

- This precision is crucial for tasks like object manipulation and spatial understanding.

3. Latency:

- Low latency is essential to ensure that virtual objects respond to user actions with minimal delay.

- High latency can break the sense of immersion and realism.

Techniques for Physical and Virtual Interactions

1. Hand and Gesture Tracking:

- Hand tracking technology allows MR systems to detect and track users' hand movements and gestures.

- This enables users to interact with virtual objects using natural hand movements.

2. Haptic Feedback:

- Haptic feedback devices provide tactile sensations to users, enhancing the sense of touch in MR interactions.

- This technology can simulate the feeling of touching or manipulating virtual objects.

3. Spatial Mapping:

- Spatial mapping involves creating a detailed 3D map of the physical environment.

- This map is used to anchor virtual objects in the real world accurately.

4. Physics Simulation:

- Implementing physics-based simulations for virtual objects allows them to behave realistically.

- Users can interact with objects as they would in the physical world, considering factors like gravity and collisions.

5. Voice Commands:

- Voice recognition technology enables users to control MR applications through spoken commands.

- This hands-free interaction method can be especially useful in scenarios where physical gestures may be challenging.

6. Object Recognition:

- MR systems can use computer vision techniques to recognize and track physical objects.

- This enables interactions between virtual objects and real-world items.

7. Gaze-based Interactions:

- Gaze tracking technology allows users to interact with virtual objects by simply looking at them.

- Users can select, manipulate, or trigger actions by directing their gaze.

Hardware Considerations

ACHIEVING NATURAL PHYSICAL and virtual interactions in MR relies on specific hardware components:

- **Tracking Sensors**: High-quality sensors for tracking head movements, hand gestures, and the physical environment are crucial for precise interactions.

- **Haptic Devices**: Haptic feedback devices, such as gloves or controllers, provide the tactile sensations necessary for realistic touch interactions.

- **Computing Power**: MR devices need powerful processors and GPUs to handle complex physics simulations and interactions in real time.

Future Developments

THE FIELD OF MR INTERACTIONS is continually evolving, with several exciting developments on the horizon:

- **Improved Hand Tracking**: Advancements in hand tracking technology will lead to more accurate and reliable interactions, including fine-grained finger tracking.

- **Wearable Haptics**: Wearable haptic devices that provide full-body feedback are being developed, further enhancing the sense of immersion.

- **AI-driven Interactions**: Machine learning algorithms will play a role in predicting user intentions and optimizing interactions.

- **Integration with IoT**: MR applications will increasingly integrate with the Internet of Things (IoT), allowing interactions with smart objects in the physical world.

In conclusion, physical and virtual interactions are at the heart of compelling MR experiences. As technology continues to advance, we can expect interactions in mixed reality to become even more natural, intuitive, and immersive.

Chapter 13: Optical and Visual Effects

Section 13.1: Understanding Human Visual System

Understanding the human visual system is crucial for creating realistic and visually appealing graphics in various applications, including video games, virtual reality, and computer-generated imagery. By gaining insights into how the human eye works, graphics professionals can optimize visual effects, rendering techniques, and display technologies to deliver immersive and visually satisfying experiences.

The Human Eye Anatomy

THE HUMAN EYE IS A complex optical system that captures and processes visual information. Key components of the human eye include:

- **Cornea**: The transparent front surface of the eye that refracts light.

- **Iris**: The colored part of the eye that controls the size of the pupil.

- **Pupil**: The aperture that regulates the amount of light entering the eye.

- **Lens**: A flexible, transparent structure that further refracts light to focus it on the retina.

- **Retina**: The innermost layer of the eye containing photoreceptor cells responsible for detecting light.

- **Optic Nerve**: Transmits visual information from the retina to the brain.

Visual Perception

UNDERSTANDING HOW THE human brain processes visual information is crucial. Some key aspects include:

1. Color Vision:

- The human eye has three types of color receptors: cones sensitive to red, green, and blue wavelengths.

- The brain processes signals from these cones to perceive a wide range of colors.

2. Spatial Resolution:

- The fovea, a small central region of the retina, provides the highest spatial resolution.

- Peripheral vision has lower resolution but a wider field of view.

3. Contrast Sensitivity:

- The ability to perceive differences in luminance (brightness) is crucial for detecting details and edges.

Visual Illusions and Perceptual Phenomena

UNDERSTANDING OPTICAL illusions and perceptual phenomena is essential for graphics professionals. These phenomena can be harnessed or mitigated for specific visual effects:

1. Depth Perception:

- Techniques like stereopsis, motion parallax, and accommodation contribute to depth perception.

- Simulating these cues can enhance the perception of 3D space in graphics.

2. Optical Illusions:

- Optical illusions, such as the Müller-Lyer illusion and Ponzo illusion, reveal how the brain interprets visual information.

- Graphics can use similar principles to create compelling illusions or distortions.

3. HDR and Tone Mapping:

- High dynamic range (HDR) rendering aims to mimic the wide range of luminance levels in the real world.

- Tone mapping techniques ensure that HDR content is viewable on standard displays.

Visual Fatigue and Comfort

GRAPHICS PROFESSIONALS must also consider the comfort and well-being of viewers:

1. Flicker and Motion Sickness:

- Rapid changes in brightness (flicker) or excessive motion can lead to discomfort or motion sickness in viewers.

- Mitigating flicker and motion issues is crucial for VR and gaming applications.

2. Color Blindness:

- Designing with colorblind users in mind is essential, as approximately 8% of men and 0.5% of women have some form of color blindness.

- Colorblind-friendly palettes and UI elements can improve accessibility.

Applying Knowledge to Graphics

UNDERSTANDING THE HUMAN visual system allows graphics professionals to:

- Optimize rendering techniques to match perceptual limitations and strengths.

- Create realistic lighting, shading, and texture effects.

- Design user interfaces that are visually clear and comfortable to use.

- Implement visual effects and illusions that enhance immersion and storytelling.

In conclusion, a deep understanding of the human visual system is fundamental for creating graphics that captivate, inform, and entertain. By leveraging this knowledge, graphics professionals can craft visual experiences that resonate with audiences across various media and applications.

Section 13.2: Optical Illusions in Graphics

OPTICAL ILLUSIONS ARE intriguing phenomena that reveal how the human visual system interprets and processes visual information. While they can sometimes deceive our perception, they are also valuable tools for graphics professionals. By understanding and harnessing optical illusions, designers and developers can create captivating and immersive visual experiences. In this section, we'll explore various optical illusions and how they can be applied in graphics.

1. Müller-Lyer Illusion

THE MÜLLER-LYER ILLUSION consists of two lines with arrow-like tails, one with inward-pointing arrows and the other with outward-pointing arrows. Even though the lines are of equal length, most people perceive the line with inward-pointing arrows as shorter than the one with outward-pointing arrows. This illusion demonstrates the role of context and perspective in visual perception.

In graphics, similar illusions can be used to create the perception of depth or size. By manipulating the surrounding elements, designers can make objects appear larger or smaller than they actually are, enhancing the 3D perception of a scene.

2. Ponzo Illusion

THE PONZO ILLUSION features two identical lines placed over converging lines that create the illusion of depth. The top line, perceived as longer, appears to be stretched to bridge the gap between the converging lines. This illusion shows how our brain uses context and perspective to estimate the size of objects.

In graphics, the Ponzo illusion's principles can be applied to create the illusion of depth and scale. By placing objects in a 3D environment with appropriate perspective cues, designers can make objects appear larger or smaller, contributing to a realistic 3D scene.

3. Kanizsa Triangle

THE KANIZSA TRIANGLE is an example of an illusory contour, where the brain perceives a contour or shape that is not explicitly defined by the stimulus. In this case, the brain perceives a white equilateral triangle in the center, even though no such triangle is present in the arrangement of Pac-Man-like shapes.

In graphics, illusory contours and shapes can be used to suggest hidden or obscured objects. This technique can be applied to create mysterious or surreal visuals, where viewers perceive shapes and structures that aren't explicitly drawn.

4. Checker Shadow Illusion

THE CHECKER SHADOW illusion is a demonstration of how lighting and context can affect our perception of color. In this illusion, two squares labeled 'A' and 'B' appear to be different shades of gray due to the shadow cast by the cylinder. However, when the background is removed, it becomes evident that both squares are the same shade.

Graphics designers can apply this concept to simulate realistic lighting conditions and shadows in virtual environments. By carefully modeling lighting and shadows, they can create the illusion of depth and differentiate between objects based on their lighting conditions.

5. Motion Illusions

OPTICAL ILLUSIONS RELATED to motion, such as the famous "rotating snakes," exploit our brain's motion processing mechanisms. These illusions create the perception of motion where none exists, leading to the sensation of objects rotating, moving, or pulsating.

In graphics and animations, simulating motion illusions can add dynamism and excitement to scenes. Techniques like motion blur, parallax scrolling, and particle systems can create the illusion of motion, enhancing the overall visual experience.

In conclusion, optical illusions are powerful tools that offer insights into the intricacies of human visual perception. Graphics professionals can leverage these illusions to create visually engaging and immersive experiences, whether in video games, virtual reality, or other forms of digital media. Understanding how the human brain interprets visual stimuli allows designers and developers to craft experiences that captivate and intrigue viewers.

Section 13.3: Physiological Effects in Graphics

GRAPHICS TECHNOLOGY has evolved significantly, and today's displays and rendering techniques are capable of producing stunning visual experiences. However, it's essential to consider the physiological effects of these visuals on viewers. This section explores various physiological aspects, including high dynamic range (HDR), color blindness, and flicker sensitivity, and how they impact graphics technology.

1. High Dynamic Range (HDR)

HDR RENDERING AND DISPLAYS offer a more extensive range of luminance and color values compared to standard dynamic range (SDR) displays. While HDR can enhance visual fidelity, it also raises concerns about potential discomfort for viewers. Bright highlights and extreme contrast can cause discomfort, especially in dark viewing environments.

To mitigate this, graphics applications should provide user-adjustable HDR settings. This allows viewers to customize the HDR experience according to their comfort level and the ambient lighting conditions. Implementing adaptive HDR tone mapping can also help maintain a comfortable viewing experience by dynamically adjusting the HDR rendering based on the environment.

2. Color Blindness

COLOR BLINDNESS IS a common visual impairment, and it's essential to consider when designing graphics and interfaces. Individuals with color vision deficiencies may have difficulty distinguishing between specific colors, which can affect their ability to perceive and interact with content.

Graphics designers should follow accessible design guidelines to ensure that their visuals are distinguishable by users with color vision deficiencies. This includes using color combinations that have sufficient contrast, providing alternative text labels for colors, and avoiding information conveyed solely through color coding.

3. Flicker Sensitivity

FLICKER SENSITIVITY refers to an individual's susceptibility to perceive flickering in screens, particularly at low refresh rates. Some people are more sensitive to flicker than others, and flickering displays can cause discomfort, eye strain, or headaches.

To address flicker sensitivity, graphics applications should offer options for adjusting refresh rates and implementing technologies like variable refresh rate (VRR). VRR synchronizes the display's refresh rate with the content's frame rate, reducing flicker and providing a smoother viewing experience.

4. Virtual Reality (VR) and Motion Sickness

VR EXPERIENCES HAVE become increasingly popular, but they can lead to motion sickness in some users. This discomfort arises due to a mismatch between the visual and vestibular systems, where the visuals suggest motion that the inner ear does not detect.

To reduce motion sickness in VR applications, developers can implement techniques like comfort modes, which reduce motion intensity or provide stationary reference points. Designers should also focus on maintaining a high and stable frame rate to minimize motion-to-photon latency, contributing to a more comfortable VR experience.

5. Eye Strain and Fatigue

EXTENDED USE OF DIGITAL displays, particularly in gaming or work environments, can lead to eye strain and fatigue. This can result from prolonged exposure to bright screens, excessive blue light emission, and insufficient rest breaks.

Graphics software should incorporate features like blue light filters and reminders for users to take regular breaks. Reducing glare, optimizing text rendering for readability, and offering adjustable font sizes can also help alleviate eye strain and fatigue.

In conclusion, graphics technology should prioritize user comfort and well-being by addressing physiological effects. Providing customization options, considering color blindness, reducing flicker, and addressing motion sickness are essential steps to ensure that visuals are not only stunning but also comfortable and inclusive for all viewers. Balancing technological advancements with user comfort is crucial in the evolving field of graphics technology.

Section 13.4: Adaptive Rendering Techniques

ADAPTIVE RENDERING techniques play a crucial role in optimizing graphics applications to provide the best possible user experience across a wide range of hardware and display conditions. These techniques involve dynamically adjusting rendering parameters and quality settings based on factors such as available hardware resources, screen resolution, and user preferences. In this section, we will explore various adaptive rendering strategies and their importance in modern graphics technology.

1. Dynamic Resolution Scaling

DYNAMIC RESOLUTION scaling, often referred to as "resolution scaling" or "dynamic resolution," is a technique where the rendering resolution is adjusted in real-time based on the GPU's load and the target frame rate. This approach allows a graphics application to maintain smooth performance even on less powerful hardware.

Implementing dynamic resolution scaling involves monitoring the frame rate and GPU usage during runtime. If the frame rate drops below the desired threshold, the application can lower the rendering resolution to reduce the GPU workload. Conversely, if there is ample GPU headroom, the resolution can be increased for improved image quality.

2. Level of Detail (LOD) Adjustment

LEVEL OF DETAIL IS a concept widely used in 3D graphics to optimize the rendering of distant or less important objects. Adaptive LOD techniques involve dynamically adjusting the level of detail for objects in the scene based on their distance from the camera and available computational resources.

By reducing the level of detail for objects that are far away from the camera or less visible, adaptive LOD ensures that the GPU spends computational resources where they are most needed. This can significantly improve performance without sacrificing visual quality.

3. Texture Streaming and Loading

TEXTURE STREAMING IS a technique commonly used in open-world games and large-scale environments. It involves loading textures and assets on-demand as the player moves through the game world. Adaptive texture streaming ensures that only the textures needed for the current scene or view frustum are loaded into memory, reducing memory consumption and load times.

Additionally, adaptive texture loading techniques prioritize textures based on their importance and visibility, ensuring that critical textures are loaded first for a seamless gaming experience.

4. Quality Presets and User Preferences

USER CUSTOMIZATION is essential in modern graphics applications. Providing quality presets and allowing users to adjust graphics settings based on their hardware and preferences is a form of adaptive rendering. Users with high-end GPUs may prefer to maximize graphical fidelity, while those with lower-end hardware may prioritize performance.

To implement this, graphics applications should offer a range of quality presets, from "Low" to "Ultra," and allow users to fine-tune individual settings such as texture quality, anti-aliasing, and shadow quality. Adaptive rendering also includes real-time adjustments when users modify these settings to ensure a smooth transition between different quality levels.

5. Environmental and Runtime Factors

ADAPTIVE RENDERING isn't limited to hardware considerations alone. Environmental factors like lighting conditions (e.g., day/night cycles) and in-game events (e.g., explosions or complex scenes) can impact rendering performance. Adaptive techniques can adjust graphical features and effects to maintain a consistent frame rate.

For example, during a night scene, a game may reduce the intensity of certain lighting effects to save GPU resources, ensuring that the game remains playable. Similarly, when a complex event occurs, the application may temporarily decrease the quality of non-essential effects to maintain responsiveness.

In summary, adaptive rendering techniques are fundamental for delivering optimal user experiences in graphics applications. These techniques consider various factors, including hardware capabilities, user preferences, and environmental conditions, to dynamically adjust rendering parameters and maintain a balance between performance and visual quality. In an ever-evolving landscape of graphics technology, adaptive rendering remains a critical aspect of achieving both stunning visuals and smooth, responsive interactions.

Section 13.5: Future of Display Technologies

THE FUTURE OF DISPLAY technologies holds immense promise, with innovations poised to transform how we interact with digital content and information. These advancements encompass a wide range of areas, from display hardware to new interaction modalities, promising more immersive and accessible experiences. In this section, we'll explore some key developments on the horizon.

1. Foldable and Rollable Displays

FOLDABLE AND ROLLABLE displays are reshaping the form factor of traditional screens. These flexible displays allow devices to transform from smartphones and tablets into larger screens or even become more compact for portability. Manufacturers are investing heavily in foldable OLED and microLED technologies, and we can expect to see more devices leveraging these displays in the near future.

Developers will need to adapt their applications to make the most of these flexible displays, creating user interfaces that intelligently adjust as screens fold, expand, or roll out. This adaptability will be crucial for ensuring a seamless user experience across different form factors.

2. Augmented Reality (AR) Glasses

AUGMENTED REALITY (AR) glasses are set to revolutionize how we perceive and interact with the digital world. Unlike virtual reality (VR), AR overlays digital information onto our view of the real world, opening up possibilities for a wide range of applications, from gaming to productivity tools.

AR glasses are becoming more compact and stylish, making them a viable consumer product. The challenge for developers will be to create engaging and useful AR experiences that seamlessly blend digital and real-world elements. This requires precise tracking, spatial mapping, and a deep understanding of user interactions.

3. 3D Holographic Displays

HOLOGRAPHIC DISPLAYS aim to bring true 3D content to life without the need for specialized glasses or headsets. Emerging technologies like light field displays and volumetric displays are making significant strides in this direction. These displays can create 3D objects that appear to exist within physical space, providing a new dimension of immersion for gaming, design, and education.

Developers will need to explore new techniques for creating content that takes full advantage of 3D holographic displays, including designing interactive 3D environments and leveraging spatial audio for a complete sensory experience.

4. Advanced Materials for Displays

THE MATERIALS USED in display technology are also evolving. Researchers are exploring novel materials like perovskite and quantum dots, which offer improved color accuracy, energy efficiency, and flexibility. These materials can enhance the vibrancy of displays while reducing their environmental impact.

Developers may need to consider the specific characteristics and requirements of these materials when optimizing content for displays that use them. Understanding the unique properties of each material can help create more visually stunning and efficient applications.

5. Eye-tracking and Biometric Feedback

EYE-TRACKING TECHNOLOGY is becoming more prevalent in both VR and AR devices. This technology allows applications to know where users are looking, enabling more natural interactions. For instance, in VR, objects can react to a user's gaze, and in AR, information can be presented precisely where the user is looking.

Biometric feedback, including measures like heart rate and skin conductance, can provide valuable insights into user experiences. Applications can adapt based on a user's emotional state or engagement level, enhancing immersion and personalization.

6. Energy-efficient Displays

AS ENVIRONMENTAL CONCERNS grow, energy-efficient display technologies are gaining importance. Low-power OLED and microLED displays, coupled with efficient rendering techniques, will be crucial for extending the battery life of mobile devices while maintaining high-quality visuals.

Developers will need to focus on optimizing graphics pipelines and content to minimize power consumption. This may involve adaptive rendering techniques that dynamically adjust rendering quality based on available power resources.

In conclusion, the future of display technologies is a vibrant landscape of innovation. Developers will play a pivotal role in harnessing the potential of these technologies to create compelling and accessible experiences. Whether it's adapting to new form factors, crafting immersive AR content, or optimizing for energy efficiency, the future of graphics programming promises exciting opportunities for those willing to embrace change and innovation.

Chapter 14: Advanced Networking and Cloud Integration

Section 14.1: Cloud-rendered Graphics

Cloud-rendered graphics represent a significant shift in the way we approach rendering for various applications, including games, simulations, and interactive media. Instead of relying solely on local hardware for rendering, cloud-rendered graphics leverage powerful remote servers to perform rendering tasks and stream the results to the user's device. This approach offers several advantages and unique challenges that we'll explore in this section.

1. On-demand Scalability

ONE OF THE PRIMARY benefits of cloud-rendered graphics is the ability to scale rendering resources on-demand. This means that applications can dynamically allocate more rendering power when needed, such as during graphically intensive scenes or in multiplayer environments with many players and complex assets.

Developers can design their applications to intelligently request additional rendering resources based on real-time performance metrics, ensuring a smooth and responsive user experience. This scalability can help maintain consistent frame rates and visual quality, even on less powerful devices.

2. Cross-platform Compatibility

CLOUD-RENDERED GRAPHICS can bridge the gap between different platforms and devices. Since the heavy lifting is done on remote servers, users can access high-quality graphics and experiences on a wide range of devices, from smartphones to low-end PCs. This approach democratizes access to graphically intensive content, making it accessible to a broader audience.

Developers need to consider how to adapt their applications to different screen sizes, input methods, and network conditions. Cross-platform compatibility becomes a crucial aspect of designing cloud-rendered graphics applications.

3. Reduced Latency Challenges

ONE OF THE MAIN CHALLENGES of cloud-rendered graphics is latency. Transmitting rendered frames from remote servers to the user's device introduces a delay that can negatively impact user interactions, especially in fast-paced applications like games.

To mitigate latency, developers can implement various techniques, such as predictive rendering and frame interpolation. Predictive rendering anticipates user input and begins rendering frames in advance, reducing the perceived delay. Frame interpolation generates intermediate frames between transmitted frames to smooth out motion.

4. Data Security and Privacy

CLOUD-RENDERED GRAPHICS involve sending user input and receiving rendered frames over the internet. This raises concerns about data security and privacy. Developers must prioritize user data protection, encryption, and secure transmission to ensure the confidentiality and integrity of user interactions and content.

Additionally, complying with data privacy regulations and user consent requirements is essential. Users should have clear information about how their data is used and the option to opt in or out of data collection.

5. Cost Management

THE SCALABILITY OF cloud-rendered graphics comes with cost implications. Developers and service providers need to manage rendering resources efficiently to avoid unnecessary expenses. This includes monitoring resource usage, optimizing rendering pipelines, and implementing cost-effective solutions.

Cost management extends to pricing models for cloud-rendered graphics services. Developers should choose pricing structures that align with their application's usage patterns and revenue model.

6. Real-time Streaming and Compression

EFFICIENT REAL-TIME streaming and compression techniques are essential for delivering cloud-rendered graphics with minimal latency and bandwidth requirements. Developers can leverage codecs optimized for real-time streaming and implement adaptive streaming protocols that adjust the quality of rendered frames based on available bandwidth.

Implementing real-time streaming and compression effectively requires a deep understanding of networking and video encoding principles.

In conclusion, cloud-rendered graphics offer exciting possibilities for creating high-quality, scalable, and cross-platform graphical experiences. While they come with challenges related to latency, data security, and cost management, addressing these challenges can lead to transformative applications that push the boundaries of what is possible in graphics programming.

Section 14.2: Real-time Stream Decomposition

REAL-TIME STREAM DECOMPOSITION is a technique used in networking and graphics programming to efficiently process and distribute streaming data, such as video and audio streams, in real-time applications. This section explores the concept of stream decomposition, its use cases, and considerations for implementing it in cloud-rendered graphics and other applications.

1. Understanding Stream Decomposition

STREAM DECOMPOSITION involves breaking down a continuous stream of data into smaller, manageable segments or packets. Each packet typically contains a portion of the data along with metadata, allowing for easy identification, organization, and processing of the content. This approach is especially useful in scenarios where data needs to be transmitted over networks with limited bandwidth and where real-time delivery is crucial.

2. Use Cases in Cloud-rendered Graphics

IN CLOUD-RENDERED GRAPHICS applications, real-time stream decomposition plays a vital role in delivering rendered frames to end-user devices. Here's how it can be applied:

- **Frame Decomposition:** Rendered frames are decomposed into smaller chunks, making it possible to transmit and render parts of a frame as they become available. This reduces perceived latency, as users can start viewing and interacting with the scene while the entire frame is being transmitted.

• **Dynamic Quality Adjustments:** Stream decomposition allows for dynamic quality adjustments based on available network bandwidth. For example, when network conditions deteriorate, the application can prioritize transmitting low-resolution or compressed segments of frames, ensuring a smoother experience.

• **Parallel Processing:** Decomposed streams can be processed in parallel, taking advantage of multicore processors and GPUs on user devices. This parallelism can enhance rendering performance and overall responsiveness.

3. Considerations for Implementation

IMPLEMENTING REAL-TIME stream decomposition requires careful planning and consideration of various factors:

• **Packet Size:** Determining the optimal packet size is crucial. Smaller packets reduce latency but increase overhead due to metadata. Larger packets may reduce overhead but can introduce perceptible delays.

• **Error Handling:** Handling lost or out-of-order packets is essential for robust stream decomposition. Implementing error detection and correction mechanisms, such as packet retransmission or forward error correction, is vital.

• **Metadata Format:** Define a standardized metadata format that includes information about each packet's content, sequence, and integrity. This metadata helps ensure proper reconstruction on the receiving end.

• **Buffer Management:** Managing buffers for incoming packets and reconstructing the original data from decomposed streams requires efficient data structures and algorithms. Developers must consider memory usage and potential bottlenecks.

• **Synchronization:** Ensure proper synchronization between decomposed streams and the rendering process on the user's device. This synchronization is crucial for maintaining a coherent and visually appealing experience.

• **Security:** Implement security measures to protect against potential attacks, such as packet injection or tampering. Encryption and authentication of decomposed streams can help maintain data integrity.

4. Real-world Applications

REAL-TIME STREAM DECOMPOSITION is not limited to cloud-rendered graphics. It finds applications in various domains, including video streaming, online gaming, teleconferencing, and remote desktop solutions. In these contexts, efficient data transmission and low-latency delivery are essential for providing seamless and responsive user experiences.

In conclusion, real-time stream decomposition is a valuable technique for optimizing data transmission in real-time applications, especially in the context of cloud-rendered graphics. When implemented thoughtfully, it can significantly improve the efficiency, responsiveness, and overall quality of user experiences in a wide range of applications.

Section 14.3: Multiplayer VR and AR Systems

MULTIPLAYER VIRTUAL Reality (VR) and Augmented Reality (AR) systems have gained significant popularity in recent years, offering immersive and collaborative experiences to users. This section delves into the challenges and techniques involved in creating multiplayer VR and AR systems, providing insights into networking, synchronization, and user interaction aspects.

1. Networking for Multiplayer VR and AR

NETWORKING IS THE BACKBONE of multiplayer VR and AR systems, enabling users to interact and share their experiences in real-time. Key considerations include:

- **Latency Management:** VR and AR systems demand low latency to maintain the illusion of presence. Implementing efficient communication protocols, minimizing data transfer, and optimizing server-client interactions are essential to achieve low-latency networking.

- **Synchronization:** Synchronizing the state of the virtual world among multiple users is challenging. Techniques such as client-side prediction and server reconciliation help maintain a consistent experience while compensating for network delays and packet loss.

- **Bandwidth Efficiency:** VR and AR experiences can be data-intensive. Optimizing data serialization, compression, and efficient use of bandwidth are crucial to prevent network congestion and ensure smooth interactions.

2. User Interaction and Collaboration

ENABLING USERS TO INTERACT with each other and the virtual world is a fundamental aspect of multiplayer VR and AR systems:

- **Avatar Representation:** Creating realistic avatars that mirror users' movements and expressions enhances the sense of presence. Techniques like full-body tracking, hand tracking, and facial expression recognition contribute to avatar fidelity.

- **Spatial Audio:** Spatial audio algorithms simulate sound propagation, enabling users to identify the direction and distance of sounds. This enhances communication and immersion, particularly in collaborative scenarios.

- **Shared Environments:** Designing shared virtual spaces where users can interact collaboratively fosters social interactions. Features like gesture recognition and object manipulation contribute to a shared sense of presence.

3. Challenges and Solutions

CREATING MULTIPLAYER VR and AR systems presents unique challenges:

- **Network Congestion:** To mitigate network congestion, developers can implement data prioritization, adaptive quality, and content caching techniques. These ensure that essential data is transmitted promptly while less critical data can be deferred or compressed.

- **Server Scalability:** As the user base grows, server scalability becomes crucial. Load balancing, cloud-based infrastructure, and dynamic server allocation can help manage increased demand.

- **Security:** Ensuring the security and privacy of user data is paramount. Implementing encryption, access control, and user authentication mechanisms prevents unauthorized access and data breaches.

- **Cross-Platform Compatibility:** Multiplayer VR and AR systems often support various devices and platforms. Developers must ensure cross-platform compatibility, enabling users with different hardware to collaborate seamlessly.

- **Content Moderation:** Preventing harassment and inappropriate behavior is essential for maintaining a positive user experience. Implementing content moderation and reporting mechanisms helps create safe virtual spaces.

4. Applications and Impact

MULTIPLAYER VR AND AR systems find applications in diverse fields, including gaming, education, telemedicine, and collaborative work environments. They enable remote collaboration, immersive training, and interactive storytelling, offering new possibilities for communication and interaction.

In conclusion, creating multiplayer VR and AR systems is a complex endeavor that requires expertise in networking, synchronization, and user interaction design. Overcoming challenges related to latency, bandwidth, and scalability is essential to provide users with immersive and collaborative experiences. As technology continues to advance, multiplayer VR and AR systems are poised to play an increasingly significant role in various domains.

Section 14.4: Server-side Physics and Logic

SERVER-SIDE PHYSICS and logic are critical components of multiplayer online games and simulations. These systems are responsible for maintaining a consistent game state across all connected clients, ensuring fair gameplay, and preventing cheating. This section explores the importance of server-side physics and logic, the challenges they present, and common techniques for their implementation.

1. Importance of Server-side Physics and Logic

IN MULTIPLAYER GAMES and simulations, client-side physics and logic can be easily manipulated or hacked. To maintain fairness and consistency, crucial game mechanics and physics simulations must be handled on the server:

- **Collision Detection:** Server-side physics ensures that collisions between game objects are accurately detected and resolved. This prevents scenarios where one player sees a different collision outcome than another.

- **Game State Synchronization:** The server is responsible for synchronizing the game state among all clients. This includes the position and movement of objects, player actions, and environmental changes.

- **Cheating Prevention:** By running critical game logic on the server, cheating attempts, such as speed hacks or teleportation, can be detected and prevented.

2. Challenges in Server-side Implementation

IMPLEMENTING SERVER-side physics and logic comes with its own set of challenges:

- **Latency:** Network latency can introduce delays in player actions and feedback. Server-side prediction and reconciliation techniques are used to minimize the impact of latency on gameplay.

- **Scalability:** As the number of players increases, server scalability becomes a concern. Load balancing and efficient server architecture are essential to accommodate a growing player base.

- **Security:** Ensuring the integrity and security of the server is crucial. Security measures, such as input validation, rate limiting, and anti-cheat mechanisms, are needed to protect against malicious actions.

- **Bandwidth Usage:** Server communication can be bandwidth-intensive. Optimizing data serialization, compression, and minimizing unnecessary data transfer are vital for efficient gameplay.

3. Techniques for Server-side Physics and Logic

SEVERAL TECHNIQUES are employed to implement server-side physics and logic:

- **Deterministic Simulation:** Using deterministic physics engines ensures that simulations produce the same results on all clients and the server. This is critical for maintaining consistency.

- **State Replication:** The server replicates essential game state information to clients. This includes player positions, object properties, and game events. Clients use this information to render the game world.

- **Client-side Prediction:** Clients predict the outcome of their actions locally to provide a responsive feel. The server reconciles these predictions with the authoritative game state to correct any deviations.

- **Physics Optimization:** On the server, physics calculations are often optimized for efficiency. This may involve simplifying collision detection or using more straightforward physics models when appropriate.

4. Applications and Impact

SERVER-SIDE PHYSICS and logic are integral to a wide range of online multiplayer games, including first-person shooters, massively multiplayer online games (MMOs), and real-time strategy games. Their implementation ensures that gameplay is fair, secure, and consistent across all players, creating a more enjoyable and competitive gaming experience.

In conclusion, server-side physics and logic are vital components of multiplayer online games and simulations. They address challenges related to fairness, security, and latency and enable the creation of engaging and competitive multiplayer experiences. As the gaming industry continues to evolve, these techniques will remain essential for maintaining the integrity and quality of online gameplay.

Section 14.5: Scalable Game Servers and Microservices

SCALABLE GAME SERVERS and microservices architecture have become increasingly prevalent in the development of modern online games. This section explores the concepts and benefits of using microservices to build scalable game server systems.

1. The Need for Scalability

ONLINE GAMES OFTEN experience fluctuating player populations and unpredictable spikes in player activity. To meet these demands, game developers require server architectures that can scale efficiently. Scalability is essential for ensuring smooth gameplay, preventing server overloads, and accommodating a growing player base.

2. Microservices Architecture

MICROSERVICES ARCHITECTURE is an approach that breaks down the monolithic structure of a game server into smaller, independent services, each responsible for a specific function. These services communicate through APIs and can be deployed and scaled independently. This architecture offers several advantages:

- **Scalability:** Microservices can be scaled individually based on demand. Critical services, such as player authentication or matchmaking, can be given more resources during peak times.

- **Faster Development:** Smaller, focused teams can work on individual microservices, leading to faster development cycles and easier maintenance.

- **Fault Isolation:** If one microservice experiences issues, it doesn't necessarily affect the entire game. This isolation improves fault tolerance and system resilience.

- **Technology Flexibility:** Different microservices can use the most suitable technology stack for their specific tasks, allowing developers to choose the right tools for the job.

3. Common Microservices in Games

SEVERAL COMMON MICROSERVICES are used in online games:

- **User Authentication:** This service handles player login and authentication, ensuring secure access to the game.

- **Matchmaking:** Matchmaking services pair players based on skill level, preferences, or other criteria to create balanced matches.

- **Game Logic:** The game logic microservice manages the core gameplay rules, including scoring, objectives, and win/lose conditions.

- **Chat and Social:** Services for in-game chat, friend lists, and player communication enhance the social aspects of gaming.

- **Analytics and Telemetry:** These microservices collect data on player behavior, allowing developers to optimize gameplay and improve the player experience.

4. Scalability Challenges

WHILE MICROSERVICES offer numerous benefits, they also present challenges:

- **Service Coordination:** Managing communication and coordination between microservices can become complex. Tools like service discovery and message brokers are used to address this.

- **Data Consistency:** Maintaining data consistency across distributed microservices can be challenging. Developers often use databases or caching solutions to synchronize data.

- **Monitoring and Debugging:** As the number of microservices grows, monitoring and debugging become more complex. Specialized tools and practices are required to ensure system health.

- **Security:** Ensuring the security of each microservice and their interactions is crucial to prevent unauthorized access and data breaches.

5. Impact on Game Development

THE ADOPTION OF MICROSERVICES architecture has a significant impact on the development process. It encourages modularity, code reusability, and a more streamlined development pipeline. However, it also requires careful planning and design to ensure effective communication between microservices and maintain system reliability.

In conclusion, scalable game servers and microservices architecture are essential components of modern online games. They enable developers to meet the demands of a dynamic player base, ensure system reliability, and deliver a smooth and enjoyable gaming experience. While adopting this approach requires careful planning and management, the benefits in terms of scalability and flexibility make it a valuable choice for game developers looking to create successful online multiplayer experiences.

Chapter 15: Security and Anti-cheat Mechanisms

Section 15.1: Understanding Common Exploits

In the world of online gaming, ensuring fair play and a secure gaming environment is crucial. Gamers expect a level playing field, and developers and operators of online games must take proactive measures to prevent various exploits and cheating mechanisms that can ruin the gaming experience. This section delves into understanding common exploits and cheating methods employed by unscrupulous players, which is the first step in devising effective anti-cheat mechanisms.

Exploits vs. Cheating

BEFORE WE DIVE INTO specific exploits, it's essential to differentiate between exploits and cheating. Exploits are unintended flaws or vulnerabilities in the game's code or design that players can take advantage of to gain an unfair advantage. Cheating, on the other hand, involves using third-party software or modifications to manipulate the game's mechanics intentionally. Both can severely impact the integrity of online games.

Wallhacks and Aimbots

WALLHACKS AND AIMBOTS are among the most common cheating tools in first-person shooters. Wallhacks allow players to see through walls and obstacles, giving them a clear view of opponents' positions. Aimbots automatically aim and shoot at enemies, often with unnaturally precise accuracy. These cheats are usually detected by monitoring players' actions for suspicious behavior.

Speed Hacks

SPEED HACKS ALTER A player's movement speed, enabling them to move faster than intended in the game. This can make a player extremely difficult to hit and provide an unfair advantage. Detecting speed hacks involves monitoring player movement patterns and flagging those who consistently move at abnormal speeds.

Exploiting Bugs and Glitches

SOME PLAYERS EXPLOIT known bugs and glitches within the game to gain advantages. This may include getting to unintended areas of the map, skipping parts of the game, or duplicating valuable in-game items. Developers must regularly patch such bugs and glitches to maintain a fair gaming environment.

DDoS Attacks

DISTRIBUTED DENIAL of Service (DDoS) attacks are not cheats within the game but are used to disrupt online gameplay. Players or groups may launch DDoS attacks against game servers to make them unavailable, causing inconvenience to other players. Mitigating DDoS attacks involves implementing robust server infrastructure and security measures.

Prevention and Detection

TO COMBAT EXPLOITS and cheating, game developers employ various prevention and detection mechanisms. These may include:

- **Anti-cheat Software**: Using third-party anti-cheat software that scans for known cheating programs and behaviors.

- **Behavior Analysis**: Monitoring player behavior for unusual patterns, such as abnormally high accuracy or impossible actions.

- **Server-side Checks**: Moving critical game logic and checks to the server to reduce the risk of client-side manipulation.

- **Regular Updates**: Consistently releasing updates and patches to fix vulnerabilities and exploits.

In conclusion, understanding common exploits and cheating methods is essential for maintaining fair play in online games. Game developers and operators must adopt a multi-faceted approach, including prevention and detection mechanisms, to create a secure and enjoyable gaming experience for all players.

Section 15.2: Secure OpenGL Programming

IN THE REALM OF GRAPHICS programming, security is often overlooked in favor of achieving the desired visual effects and performance. However, writing secure OpenGL code is of paramount importance, especially in contexts where user-generated content or external data can be loaded into a rendering pipeline. This section explores best practices for secure OpenGL programming, focusing on mitigating common security vulnerabilities.

Input Validation

ONE OF THE PRIMARY sources of security vulnerabilities in OpenGL programs is insufficient input validation. When loading textures, shaders, or other assets from external sources, it's crucial to validate and sanitize input data thoroughly. Failure to do so can lead to buffer overflows, memory corruption, or even remote code execution.

Here's an example of loading a texture in OpenGL with input validation:

```
GLuint LoadTexture(const char* filename) {

if (!filename || strlen(filename) == 0) {

// Invalid input, don't proceed

return 0;

}

// Load and validate the texture file

// ...

return textureID;

}
```

Shader Security

SHADERS ARE POWERFUL tools in OpenGL, but they can also introduce security risks if not handled properly. Avoid using user-generated or untrusted shader code, as it can execute arbitrary operations on the GPU, potentially compromising the system's security.

If you must use user-generated shaders, consider using a restricted shader language or sandboxing the execution environment to limit potential damage. Additionally, validate and sanitize shader inputs to prevent malicious code injection.

Memory Safety

OPENGL CODE OFTEN DEALS with buffers and memory allocations. It's essential to follow best practices for memory safety to prevent buffer overflows and other memory-related vulnerabilities. Use functions like glBufferData and glBufferSubData to ensure that data fits within the allocated buffer.

Here's an example of using glBufferData safely:

GLuint buffer;

size_t bufferSize = /* *Calculate buffer size* */;

void* data = /* *Your data* */;

glGenBuffers(1, &buffer);

glBindBuffer(GL_ARRAY_BUFFER, buffer);

glBufferData(GL_ARRAY_BUFFER,   bufferSize,   data, GL_STATIC_DRAW);

Shader Compilation and Linking

DURING SHADER COMPILATION and linking, it's essential to check for errors and handle them gracefully. Inadequate error checking can lead to undefined behavior and security vulnerabilities. Always verify shader compilation and linking status and log any errors for debugging purposes.

```
GLuint vertexShader = /* Compile vertex shader */;

GLuint fragmentShader = /* Compile fragment shader */;

GLuint shaderProgram = glCreateProgram();

glAttachShader(shaderProgram, vertexShader);

glAttachShader(shaderProgram, fragmentShader);

glLinkProgram(shaderProgram);

// Check for linking errors

GLint linked;

glGetProgramiv(shaderProgram, GL_LINK_STATUS, &linked);

if (!linked) {

GLint logLength;

glGetProgramiv(shaderProgram,      GL_INFO_LOG_LENGTH,
&logLength);

if (logLength > 0) {

GLchar* log = (GLchar*)malloc(logLength);

glGetProgramInfoLog(shaderProgram, logLength, NULL, log);

// Handle the error log

free(log);

}

// Handle the linking error

}
```

Resource Management

PROPER RESOURCE MANAGEMENT is essential for security and performance. Ensure that OpenGL resources like textures, buffers, and shaders are correctly deleted when they are no longer needed. Resource leaks can lead to memory exhaustion and potential security vulnerabilities.

// Delete a texture when it's no longer needed

glDeleteTextures(1, &textureID);

By following these best practices for secure OpenGL programming, you can minimize the risk of security vulnerabilities and ensure the stability and reliability of your graphics applications. Security should be a fundamental consideration, alongside visual quality and performance, in any OpenGL project.

Section 15.3: Anti-cheat Techniques and Mechanisms

IN THE WORLD OF ONLINE gaming, maintaining a fair and enjoyable experience for all players is paramount. Anti-cheat mechanisms are essential tools used by game developers to combat cheating and ensure fair play. This section delves into various anti-cheat techniques and mechanisms commonly employed in online multiplayer games.

Client-Side Anti-Cheat Measures

1. Code Obfuscation

GAME DEVELOPERS OFTEN use code obfuscation techniques to make it more challenging for cheaters to reverse-engineer and modify game code. This involves renaming variables and functions and inserting dummy code to confuse potential cheaters. While code obfuscation is not foolproof, it adds an extra layer of complexity for would-be cheaters.

// Before obfuscation

int playerScore = 1000;

// After obfuscation

int a1f5g7h3k2 = 1000;

2. Client-Side Validation

CLIENT-SIDE VALIDATION involves checking game events and actions on the player's device before they are sent to the game server. This can help detect and prevent certain types of cheats, such as speed hacks or aimbots. However, it's essential to balance client-side validation with server-side validation to avoid false positives.

// Client-side speed validation

if (playerSpeed > MAX_SPEED) {

playerSpeed = MAX_SPEED;

}

Server-Side Anti-Cheat Mechanisms

1. Server Authority

IN A TRUSTED SERVER model, the game server has the ultimate authority over the game state. Clients can send their actions, but the server verifies and enforces the rules. This prevents clients from manipulating game data directly and ensures fair play.

```
// Server-side validation of player movement

if (IsValidMove(playerPosition, newPlayerPosition)) {

UpdatePlayerPosition(newPlayerPosition);

}
```

2. Player Behavior Analysis

MANY MODERN ANTI-CHEAT systems use behavioral analysis to detect suspicious player behavior. This involves collecting data on player actions and patterns over time and flagging or banning players who exhibit unusual or impossible behavior.

```
// Behavior analysis: Detecting aimbot-like behavior

if (IsAimbotDetected(player)) {

BanPlayer(player);

}
```

3. Data Encryption

ENCRYPTING GAME DATA during transmission between the client and server can prevent data manipulation by cheaters. This is particularly important for sensitive data like player scores or in-game currency.

```
// Encrypting player score data before transmission

encryptedScore = EncryptData(playerScore);
```

SendEncryptedScoreToServer(encryptedScore);

Reporting and Community Involvement

1. Reporting Systems

IMPLEMENTING IN-GAME reporting systems empowers players to report suspected cheaters. Developers can then review these reports and take action against confirmed cheaters, such as banning their accounts.

2. Community Moderation

ENGAGING THE COMMUNITY in the fight against cheaters can be effective. Some games have volunteer moderators who review reports and monitor gameplay. This collaborative approach can help maintain a fair gaming environment.

Continuous Improvement

ANTI-CHEAT MECHANISMS must evolve continuously to stay ahead of cheaters who are constantly developing new methods to exploit games. Regular updates and patches that address vulnerabilities and adapt to new cheating techniques are essential.

In conclusion, anti-cheat techniques and mechanisms play a vital role in maintaining fair and enjoyable online gaming experiences. Developers must strike a balance between client-side and server-side measures, employ behavioral analysis, and involve the gaming community in reporting and moderation. By staying vigilant and continuously improving anti-cheat systems, game developers can create a more secure and enjoyable multiplayer environment.

Section 15.4: Encrypted Networking in Games

SECURE COMMUNICATION is crucial in online gaming to protect player data, prevent cheating, and ensure a fair and enjoyable gaming experience. Encrypted networking is a fundamental component of securing game traffic between players and servers. This section explores the importance of encrypted networking in games and how it can be implemented.

The Need for Encrypted Networking

Protecting Player Data

IN ONLINE GAMES, PLAYER data, including login credentials, in-game transactions, and personal information, must be kept confidential. Encrypted networking ensures that sensitive data cannot be intercepted and read by malicious actors during transmission.

Preventing Cheating

ENCRYPTION ALSO PLAYS a role in preventing cheating. Without proper encryption, malicious players can intercept and manipulate game data packets, potentially giving them unfair advantages or disrupting the gameplay experience for others.

Implementing Encryption Protocols

SSL/TLS (Secure Sockets Layer/Transport Layer Security)

SSL/TLS IS A WIDELY used encryption protocol that establishes a secure and encrypted connection between a client (player) and a server. It ensures data confidentiality and integrity during transmission. Most online games use SSL/TLS to encrypt data, including login information and in-game communications.

 # Python code using the `requests` library with SSL/TLS

import requests

 # Send a secure HTTP request

response = requests.get("https://example.com", verify=True)

Encryption of Game Traffic

IN ADDITION TO SECURING player data, game-related traffic, such as player positions, actions, and game events, should also be encrypted. This prevents attackers from eavesdropping on or tampering with the gameplay.

// C++ code using encryption for game traffic

EncryptAndSendGameData(playerPosition, gameEvent);

Public Key Infrastructure (PKI)

MANY ONLINE GAMES USE a Public Key Infrastructure (PKI) to manage encryption keys. PKI involves the use of public and private keys to secure data. The server has a public key for encrypting data, and only it possesses the corresponding private key for decryption.

// Java code demonstrating PKI encryption

PublicKey serverPublicKey = loadServerPublicKey();

```
byte[] encryptedData = encryptWithPublicKey(serverPublicKey,
gameData);
```

Challenges and Considerations

Latency

ENCRYPTING AND DECRYPTING data adds a slight overhead in terms of processing time. While modern encryption methods are efficient, minimizing latency remains a consideration for real-time games where low latency is crucial.

Key Management

MANAGING ENCRYPTION keys is essential. Keys must be kept secure, rotated regularly, and only accessible to authorized personnel. Key management is critical to maintaining the integrity of the encryption system.

Conclusion

ENCRYPTED NETWORKING is a cornerstone of secure online gaming. It protects player data, prevents cheating, and helps maintain the integrity of the gameplay experience. Game developers must implement encryption protocols like SSL/TLS, secure game traffic, and manage encryption keys effectively to ensure a safe and enjoyable gaming environment for all players.

Section 15.5: Forensics and Post-breach Analysis

IN THE WORLD OF ONLINE gaming, security breaches and incidents can happen despite best efforts to protect game environments. When such incidents occur, forensics and post-breach analysis become vital processes to understand what went wrong, assess the extent of the breach, and take appropriate actions to mitigate damage and prevent future incidents.

The Importance of Post-breach Analysis

Understanding the Attack

POST-BREACH ANALYSIS helps game developers and security teams understand how an attack occurred. This includes identifying the attack vector, entry points, and the methods used by the attacker. This knowledge is crucial for closing vulnerabilities and improving security.

Assessing the Impact

ANALYZING THE BREACH allows teams to assess the impact on players, their accounts, and the game environment. Understanding the scope of the breach helps in determining the appropriate response, such as notifying affected players or resetting compromised accounts.

Incident Response Plan

Developing a Response Plan

A WELL-DEFINED INCIDENT response plan is essential for handling security breaches efficiently. This plan outlines the steps to take when a breach is detected, including who to notify, how to contain the breach, and how to recover from it.

 # Sample incident response plan (YAML)

incident_plan:

- Detection: Immediately detect and report any security breach.

- Containment: Isolate affected systems to prevent further damage.

- Notification: Notify affected players and relevant authorities.

- Investigation: Analyze the breach to understand the attack.

- Recovery: Implement security patches and measures to recover.

- Communication: Keep players informed about the situation.

- Evaluation: Assess the incident response and make improvements.

Simulating Breach Scenarios

REGULARLY SIMULATING breach scenarios through penetration testing and red teaming exercises can help teams practice their incident response plans and uncover vulnerabilities before malicious attackers do.

Digital Forensics

Gathering Evidence

DIGITAL FORENSICS INVOLVES collecting and analyzing digital evidence related to a security breach. This evidence can include log files, network traffic data, and system snapshots. Analyzing this data helps in identifying the extent of the breach and the attacker's actions.

 # Shell command for examining log files

grep "suspicious_activity" /var/log/game_server.log

Chain of Custody

MAINTAINING A SECURE chain of custody for digital evidence is critical. It ensures that the evidence is preserved, protected from tampering, and admissible in legal proceedings if necessary.

Learning from Incidents

Continuous Improvement

EVERY SECURITY INCIDENT should be seen as an opportunity for improvement. Game developers and security teams should conduct post-incident reviews to identify weaknesses in their security posture and take measures to strengthen it.

Sharing Knowledge

SHARING KNOWLEDGE ABOUT security incidents within the gaming industry is essential. It helps other game developers learn from past incidents and enhance their security practices.

Conclusion

WHILE ROBUST SECURITY measures are crucial for preventing security breaches, it's equally important to be prepared for incidents. Forensics and post-breach analysis enable game developers to respond effectively, learn from their experiences, and continually improve the security of online gaming environments. By doing so, they can provide players with safer and more enjoyable gaming experiences.

Chapter 16: Toolchain and Workflow Mastery

In the world of graphics programming, mastering your toolchain and workflow is essential for creating efficient, high-quality, and visually stunning applications. This chapter explores advanced techniques and practices that can streamline your development process, improve debugging capabilities, and enhance collaboration among team members.

Section 16.1: Advanced Debugging Techniques

DEBUGGING IS AN INTEGRAL part of the development process, helping you identify and rectify issues in your graphics applications. While basic debugging tools are invaluable, advanced debugging techniques can take your debugging skills to the next level.

Profiling and Performance Analysis

PROFILING TOOLS ALLOW you to examine the performance of your graphics application in detail. These tools provide insights into CPU and GPU usage, memory allocation, and frame rendering times. By identifying performance bottlenecks, you can optimize critical sections of your code for better frame rates and responsiveness.

 # Python example using a profiling library

import cProfile

```
def expensive_function():
```

 # Code with potential performance issues

```
pass
```

```
cProfile.run("expensive_function()")
```

Real-time Debugging

REAL-TIME DEBUGGING tools enable you to inspect and modify your application's state while it's running. These tools often come with integrated development environments (IDEs) and allow you to set breakpoints, step through code, and inspect variable values during runtime.

// C++ example using a debugger

```
#include <iostream>
```

```
int main() {
```

```
int x = 42;
```

```
std::cout << "The value of x is: " << x << std::endl;
```

// Set a breakpoint here and inspect variable values

```
return 0;
```

```
}
```

Memory Analysis

MEMORY ANALYSIS TOOLS help you detect and resolve memory-related issues such as memory leaks and excessive memory consumption. These tools provide detailed reports on memory allocation and deallocation patterns, allowing you to identify memory leaks and optimize memory usage.

```java
// Java example using a memory profiler

public class MemoryLeakExample {

public static void main(String[] args) {

while (true) {

// Allocate memory without releasing it

String data = new String(new byte[1024]);

}

}

}
```

Integration with Graphics Debugging Tools

GRAPHICS DEBUGGING tools, like NVIDIA Nsight and RenderDoc, enable you to inspect the rendering pipeline, view GPU resources, and diagnose rendering issues. Integrating these tools into your workflow can help you identify rendering artifacts, shader errors, and resource management problems.

Collaborative Debugging

COLLABORATIVE DEBUGGING involves multiple team members working together to identify frand resolve issues efficiently. Version control systems (e.g., Git) and collaborative debugging platforms (e.g., Visual Studio Live Share) facilitate teamwork by allowing developers to share code and debug sessions in real-time.

Continuous Integration (CI)

INCORPORATING CI SYSTEMS into your workflow automates the building, testing, and deployment of your graphics applications. CI pipelines can include automated code reviews, static analysis, and regression testing, ensuring that new code changes do not introduce bugs or performance regressions.

 # Sample CI/CD pipeline (YAML)

stages:

- build

- test

- deploy

 # Define jobs for each stage

Live Coding and Hot Reloading

LIVE CODING AND HOT reloading tools, like Unreal Engine's Blueprints and Unity's Play Mode, enable developers to make code changes while the application is running. This rapid iteration process accelerates development and debugging, allowing you to see the immediate effects of code modifications.

Code and Asset Pipelining

EFFICIENT ASSET AND code management is critical in large graphics projects. Implementing robust pipelines for code compilation, shader generation, and asset import/export can improve productivity and ensure consistency across the development team.

Conclusion

MASTERING YOUR TOOLCHAIN and workflow is essential for achieving success in graphics programming. Advanced debugging techniques, collaboration tools, and automation practices can significantly enhance your development process, enabling you to create visually impressive graphics applications efficiently.

Section 16.2: Continuous Integration for Graphics Projects

CONTINUOUS INTEGRATION (CI) is a software development practice that plays a crucial role in maintaining the quality, stability, and efficiency of graphics projects. In this section, we will explore how CI can be tailored to the specific needs of graphics development, helping you catch issues early, ensure consistent builds, and collaborate effectively within a team.

The Basics of Continuous Integration

AT ITS CORE, CI IS about automatically building, testing, and validating your code with each change you make to your project's repository. CI systems monitor your version control system (e.g., Git) for any new commits and trigger a series of predefined tasks.

These tasks typically include:

1. **Code Compilation:** Building your graphics application, shaders, and associated tools.
2. **Unit Testing:** Running automated tests to ensure that individual parts of your code work as expected.
3. **Integration Testing:** Checking how different parts of your application work together.
4. **Static Code Analysis:** Scanning your codebase for

potential issues, such as code style violations and potential bugs.

5. **Deployment:** Preparing the application for deployment or distribution.

Benefits of CI in Graphics Development

CI BRINGS SEVERAL ADVANTAGES to graphics development:

1. Early Issue Detection: CI pipelines automatically build and test code changes, identifying errors and regressions early in the development process, reducing the time and effort needed to diagnose and fix issues.

2. Consistency: CI ensures that all team members work with the same codebase and build processes, reducing compatibility issues and enhancing collaboration.

3. Collaboration: CI systems often include features for code review and collaboration, allowing team members to discuss and approve changes before they are merged into the main codebase.

4. Continuous Deployment: For applications that are continuously deployed, CI can automate the deployment process, ensuring that the latest stable version is always available.

Setting Up CI for Graphics Projects

HERE'S A HIGH-LEVEL overview of how you can set up CI for your graphics project:

1. Choose a CI Service: There are several CI services available, such as Jenkins, Travis CI, CircleCI, GitLab CI/CD, and GitHub Actions. Select the one that best fits your project's requirements and integrates well with your version control system.

2. Define a CI Configuration: Create a configuration file (e.g., .travis.yml or .gitlab-ci.yml) in your project's repository. This file outlines the steps to build, test, and deploy your application.

3. Configure Build Environments: Specify the build environment, including the operating system, compilers, and dependencies needed for your graphics project. This ensures that the CI system can accurately replicate your development environment.

4. Set Up Testing: Define unit tests and integration tests for your graphics code. CI will automatically run these tests whenever changes are pushed to the repository.

5. Integration with Graphics Debugging Tools: If you use graphics debugging tools like RenderDoc or NVIDIA Nsight, consider integrating them into your CI pipeline to automatically identify rendering issues.

6. Automatic Deployment: For projects that require continuous deployment, configure your CI pipeline to deploy the application to the desired platforms or distribution channels.

Example CI Configuration (Travis CI)

```yaml
# .TRAVIS.YML

language: cpp

os: linux

dist: focal

before_install:

- sudo apt-get update -qq

- sudo apt-get install -y libglfw3-dev # Install required libraries
```

script:

- make build *# Replace with your build script*

- make test *# Replace with your test script*

Monitoring and Notifications

CI SYSTEMS TYPICALLY provide notifications through email, messaging platforms, or other communication channels. Configure notifications to alert your team when build or test failures occur, ensuring that issues are addressed promptly.

Conclusion

CONTINUOUS INTEGRATION is a valuable practice for graphics development, enhancing code quality, collaboration, and the efficiency of your project. By automating essential tasks, you can focus more on creating stunning graphics and less on debugging and build issues.

Section 16.3: Shader and Asset Pipelining

SHADER AND ASSET PIPELINING is a critical aspect of graphics development, enabling efficient management, compilation, and deployment of shaders and game assets. In this section, we will delve into the importance of a robust pipeline for shaders and assets in graphics projects and explore best practices for implementation.

The Significance of Shader and Asset Pipelining

IN GRAPHICS DEVELOPMENT, shaders and assets play a pivotal role in creating visually stunning and immersive experiences. However, managing shaders and assets efficiently is often a complex challenge due to the following reasons:

1. **Variety of Assets:** Graphics projects involve a wide range of assets, including 3D models, textures, materials, shaders, and more.
2. **Multiple Platforms:** To reach a broader audience, graphics applications often need to run on various platforms, each with its specific requirements.
3. **Constant Iteration:** Developers frequently iterate on shaders and assets to achieve the desired visual quality and performance.

A well-structured shader and asset pipeline addresses these challenges, streamlining the development process and ensuring that assets are optimized for real-time rendering.

Key Components of a Shader and Asset Pipeline

1. Asset Importers

ASSET IMPORTERS ARE responsible for translating various asset formats (e.g., FBX, OBJ, PNG, JPEG) into a format that is optimized for real-time rendering. These importers should be able to handle asset transformations, such as scaling and rotation, and generate data structures that can be easily consumed by the rendering engine.

2. Shader Compilation

SHADERS ARE TYPICALLY written in high-level languages like GLSL or HLSL. A shader compiler translates these high-level shaders into a format that can be executed by the GPU. Your pipeline should automate the compilation process, ensuring that shaders are compatible with the target platform and hardware.

3. Asset Compression

GRAPHICS ASSETS, ESPECIALLY textures and 3D models, can consume a significant amount of memory. Asset compression techniques, such as texture compression and mesh optimization, can significantly reduce memory usage without sacrificing visual quality. Integrating asset compression into your pipeline is crucial for efficient resource utilization.

4. Dependency Management

AS YOUR PROJECT GROWS, managing dependencies between assets and shaders becomes more challenging. A pipeline should track these dependencies and update assets and shaders automatically when their source files change. This ensures that your project stays up-to-date and minimizes the chances of runtime errors.

5. Platform-Specific Compilation

DIFFERENT PLATFORMS may require platform-specific shader and asset configurations. Your pipeline should be capable of generating platform-specific builds, allowing you to optimize assets and shaders for each target platform.

Implementing a Shader and Asset Pipeline

HERE'S A SIMPLIFIED example of a shader and asset pipeline using Python and a hypothetical graphics framework:

 # Asset Importer

```
def import_model(model_file):
```

```python
# Import the 3D model and perform necessary transformations
return optimized_model_data

def import_texture(texture_file):
# Import the texture and apply compression
return compressed_texture_data

# Shader Compilation
def compile_shader(shader_code, platform):
# Compile the shader code for the specified platform
return compiled_shader_code

# Asset Compression
def compress_texture(texture_data):
# Apply texture compression algorithms
return compressed_texture_data

def optimize_mesh(model_data):
# Apply mesh optimization techniques
return optimized_model_data

# Dependency Management
def track_dependencies(asset, shader):
# Track dependencies between assets and shaders
pass
```

 # Platform-Specific Compilation

def generate_platform_specific_build(asset, shader, platform):

 # Generate platform-specific asset and shader builds

pass

This example illustrates the basic structure of a shader and asset pipeline, but in practice, pipelines can become much more complex depending on the project's size and requirements.

Benefits of a Robust Pipeline

A WELL-IMPLEMENTED shader and asset pipeline offers several advantages:

- **Efficiency:** Developers can focus on creating assets and shaders without worrying about manual optimization and compilation tasks, saving time and reducing errors.

- **Consistency:** Assets and shaders are consistently optimized and compiled, ensuring that the application runs smoothly on different platforms.

- **Scalability:** As your project grows, a pipeline allows you to manage a large number of assets and shaders efficiently.

- **Cross-Platform Compatibility:** A pipeline can generate platform-specific builds, ensuring compatibility with various target platforms.

In conclusion, a robust shader and asset pipeline is essential for graphics development. It streamlines asset and shader management, improves efficiency, and ensures that your graphics project looks and performs its best across different platforms.

Section 16.4: Live Coding and Hot Reloading

LIVE CODING AND HOT reloading are powerful techniques in graphics development that enhance productivity and streamline the iterative process of creating and fine-tuning shaders, rendering techniques, and other real-time components of graphics applications.

What is Live Coding?

LIVE CODING, OFTEN referred to as interactive coding, allows developers to modify and experiment with code in real time while the application is running. This approach provides instant feedback on changes, making it particularly valuable for graphics development where visual results are crucial.

The Benefits of Live Coding

1. Rapid Iteration

LIVE CODING ENABLES developers to iterate quickly on graphics features. You can adjust shader parameters, lighting, materials, and other aspects of the scene and immediately see the results, facilitating a faster development cycle.

2. Real-time Debugging

WITH LIVE CODING, YOU can insert debug statements or visual overlays directly into your scene. This helps identify issues and inspect variables without interrupting the application's execution.

3. Visual Feedback

DEVELOPERS CAN VISUALIZE complex data structures, algorithms, or procedural generation in real time. This is particularly useful when working on effects like particle systems, dynamic simulations, or procedural content generation.

4. Experimentation

LIVE CODING ENCOURAGES experimentation. Developers can try out different ideas, techniques, or configurations without the need for a full rebuild or restarting the application, making it easier to explore creative possibilities.

Implementing Live Coding

IMPLEMENTING LIVE CODING typically involves the following steps:

1. Code Injection

YOUR GRAPHICS APPLICATION should be designed to accept code injections. This code can be in the form of shader code, scripting, or configuration files.

2. Hot Reloading

HOT RELOADING IS THE process of injecting code changes into the running application without stopping or restarting it. This can be achieved using libraries or frameworks that support dynamic reloading.

3. User Interface Integration

DEVELOPERS OFTEN CREATE a user interface (UI) for live coding, allowing them to adjust parameters, reload shaders, or trigger specific actions in real time.

Here's a simplified example in Python using Pygame to demonstrate live coding with hot reloading:

```python
import pygame

import hotreload

# Initialize Pygame and create a window

pygame.init()

screen = pygame.display.set_mode((800, 600))

# Define a simple shader function

shader_code = """

void main() {

gl_FragColor = vec4(1.0, 0.0, 0.0, 1.0); // Red color

}

"""
```

```python
# Hot reload the shader code

@hotreload.watch

def load_shader():

return shader_code

def main():

running = True

shader = None

while running:

for event in pygame.event.get():

if event.type == pygame.QUIT:

running = False

# Reload the shader code if it has changed

new_shader_code = load_shader()

if new_shader_code != shader_code:

shader_code = new_shader_code

shader = compile_shader(shader_code)

# Render the scene using the current shader

if shader:

render_with_shader(shader)

pygame.display.flip()
```

```
pygame.quit()

if __name__ == "__main__":

main()
```

In this example, the hotreload library is used to monitor changes in the shader_code and automatically reload it when modified.

Challenges of Live Coding

WHILE LIVE CODING OFFERS many benefits, it comes with challenges:

- **Complexity:** Implementing a robust live coding system can be complex, particularly for large and complex graphics applications.

- **Performance Overhead:** Continuous code reloading can introduce performance overhead, especially when dealing with large shaders or assets.

- **Debugging:** Debugging live code can be more challenging due to the dynamic nature of changes and potential side effects.

Despite these challenges, live coding is a valuable tool for graphics developers, enabling them to achieve faster development cycles and more creative experimentation in real-time rendering projects.

Section 16.5: Collaborative Tools and Techniques

COLLABORATION IS AN essential aspect of modern graphics development, as it allows multiple developers, artists, and designers to work together seamlessly on complex projects. In this section, we will explore various collaborative tools and techniques that facilitate teamwork and enhance productivity in graphics programming.

Version Control Systems (VCS)

1. Git and GitHub: Git is a distributed version control system widely used in the software development industry. Platforms like GitHub provide hosting for Git repositories, making it easy for teams to collaborate on code. Version control enables developers to track changes, merge contributions, and manage project history effectively.

Integrated Development Environments (IDEs)

2. Visual Studio Code (VS Code): VS Code is a popular code editor with robust support for extensions and integrated version control. Extensions like Live Share allow multiple developers to collaboratively edit code in real time, making it a powerful choice for graphics development teams.

Collaboration Platforms

3. Slack and Microsoft Teams: These communication platforms facilitate real-time messaging, file sharing, and collaboration among team members. Graphics teams can use these tools to discuss ideas, share progress, and provide feedback efficiently.

Cloud-Based Services

4. Cloud Storage: Services like Google Drive, Dropbox, and OneDrive offer cloud storage for graphics assets and project files.

This ensures that team members can access the latest resources from anywhere with an internet connection.

5. Google Workspace and Microsoft 365: These productivity suites provide tools for document collaboration, such as Google Docs and Microsoft Word Online. They enable multiple users to work on documents simultaneously, making them useful for project documentation.

Collaborative Development Practices

6. Code Reviews: Implementing a code review process allows team members to review each other's code for quality, correctness, and adherence to coding standards. Tools like GitHub's pull requests facilitate code reviews.

7. Pair Programming: In pair programming, two developers work together at the same computer. This practice can lead to faster problem-solving and knowledge sharing within the team.

8. Regular Meetings: Scheduled meetings, such as stand-ups or sprint retrospectives, provide opportunities for team members to sync up, discuss progress, and address challenges.

Collaborative Graphics Workflows

9. Asset Pipelines: Establishing well-defined asset pipelines ensures that artists and designers can seamlessly integrate their work into the development process. Tools like Adobe Creative Cloud and Blender can be integrated with version control systems to manage graphical assets efficiently.

10. Shader Libraries: Maintaining a library of reusable shaders and materials can streamline the graphics development process. Team members can contribute to and benefit from this shared resource.

11. Documentation: Comprehensive documentation of graphics techniques, asset formats, and coding standards is crucial for enabling smooth collaboration. Documentation should be kept up to date and easily accessible to all team members.

Challenges of Collaboration

WHILE COLLABORATION is vital, it can also present challenges:

- **Communication:** Effective communication is crucial in a collaborative environment. Misunderstandings or lack of clear communication can lead to errors and delays.

- **Integration:** Integrating assets and code from various team members can be complex, particularly in large projects with multiple contributors.

- **Consistency:** Maintaining consistency in coding style, asset naming conventions, and design choices is essential for a cohesive final product.

- **Conflict Resolution:** Conflicts can arise when team members have differing opinions or make changes that affect each other's work. Conflict resolution strategies should be in place to address these issues promptly.

In conclusion, collaborative tools and techniques are essential for graphics development teams to work efficiently and produce high-quality results. By using version control systems, communication platforms, cloud services, and collaborative development practices, teams can overcome challenges and create impressive graphics projects together.

Chapter 17: Integrating Emerging Technologies

Section 17.1: Quantum Computing and Graphics

Quantum computing is a rapidly advancing field that has the potential to revolutionize various domains, including graphics and simulations. In this section, we will explore the intersection of quantum computing and graphics, discussing the fundamentals, potential applications, and challenges involved.

Understanding Quantum Computing

QUANTUM COMPUTING LEVERAGES the principles of quantum mechanics to perform computations that are currently beyond the capabilities of classical computers. Unlike classical bits, which can represent either a 0 or a 1, quantum bits or qubits can exist in multiple states simultaneously due to superposition. This property allows quantum computers to handle complex problems more efficiently.

Potential Applications in Graphics

1. Quantum Simulations: Quantum computers can simulate physical phenomena with incredible precision. In graphics, this means the ability to model complex materials, lighting, and particle interactions more accurately. This can lead to highly realistic simulations and visual effects.

2. Optimization: Quantum computing excels in optimization tasks. Graphics rendering involves numerous optimization challenges, such as ray tracing and path tracing. Quantum algorithms could potentially optimize these processes, reducing rendering times.

3. Machine Learning: Quantum machine learning algorithms have shown promise in solving complex problems. In graphics, this could lead to advancements in AI-driven content creation, style transfer, and animation.

Challenges and Limitations

WHILE THE POTENTIAL benefits are exciting, quantum computing in graphics faces several challenges:

1. Hardware Limitations: Quantum computers are still in their infancy, with limited qubits and stability. Building practical quantum hardware for graphics tasks remains a significant challenge.

2. Algorithm Development: Developing quantum algorithms for graphics tasks is complex and requires expertise in both quantum computing and computer graphics. This limits the number of researchers who can contribute effectively.

3. Integration Complexity: Integrating quantum computing into existing graphics pipelines and software is not straightforward. It requires specialized knowledge and tools.

Quantum Computing Tools for Graphics

DEVELOPERS INTERESTED in exploring quantum computing for graphics should consider the following tools and resources:

1. Quantum Development Kits (QDKs): QDKs, such as Microsoft's Quantum Development Kit, provide the tools and libraries needed to experiment with quantum algorithms. These kits include simulators for quantum computations.

2. Quantum Cloud Services: Cloud providers like IBM and Amazon offer access to quantum computers through cloud platforms, making it easier for developers to experiment with quantum algorithms without investing in quantum hardware.

Future Outlook

THE INTEGRATION OF quantum computing into graphics is a long-term goal. As quantum hardware becomes more accessible and stable, and as quantum algorithms for graphics tasks are developed, we can expect to see exciting advancements in rendering, simulations, and AI-driven graphics content creation.

In conclusion, quantum computing holds great promise for the field of computer graphics. While challenges remain, the potential benefits in terms of more realistic simulations, faster rendering, and advanced AI-driven graphics are worth exploring. Developers interested in this emerging field should keep an eye on advancements in quantum computing and its applications in graphics.

Section 17.2: Integrating Biometrics in Games

INTEGRATING BIOMETRICS, which involves the measurement and analysis of human physiological and behavioral traits, into video games is an emerging trend that can enhance player experiences and gameplay mechanics. In this section, we will explore the potential applications, benefits, and considerations of integrating biometric data into games.

Understanding Biometrics in Gaming

BIOMETRIC DATA INCLUDES information about a player's physiological state, such as heart rate, skin conductance, eye movements, and more. By capturing and analyzing this data, game developers can gain insights into a player's emotional and cognitive responses during gameplay.

Potential Applications

1. Adaptive Gameplay: Biometrics can be used to adjust the difficulty or intensity of the game in real-time based on the player's stress levels or engagement. For example, if a player's heart rate indicates high stress, the game can reduce the number of enemies or provide assistance.

2. Narrative Adaptation: Biometrics can influence the game's storyline or events. If a player's emotional response suggests boredom or frustration, the game can introduce plot twists or challenges to re-engage the player.

3. Health and Fitness Games: Biometrics can play a central role in health and fitness games. Games can track a player's heart rate during workouts and provide feedback on performance and progress.

Benefits of Biometric Integration

1. Enhanced Immersion: Biometrics can make games more immersive by adapting to the player's emotional state, making the experience feel more personalized and responsive.

2. Player Insights: Game developers can gain valuable insights into how players react to different game elements, helping them refine gameplay mechanics and storytelling.

3. Health and Well-being: Biometric games can promote physical and mental well-being by encouraging players to be more aware of their physiological responses.

Considerations and Challenges

1. Privacy Concerns: Collecting biometric data raises privacy and ethical concerns. Game developers must ensure they comply with data protection regulations and obtain informed consent from players.

2. Accuracy and Reliability: Biometric sensors must be accurate and reliable to provide meaningful data. Calibration and testing are essential.

3. Interpretation: Analyzing biometric data can be complex. Developers need to determine how to interpret the data and translate it into meaningful gameplay adjustments.

Tools and Technologies

DEVELOPERS INTERESTED in integrating biometrics into games can explore various tools and technologies:

1. Biometric Sensors: Devices like heart rate monitors, eye-tracking cameras, and skin conductance sensors can capture biometric data.

2. Biometric Software Libraries: There are software libraries and APIs available that facilitate the integration of biometric data into game engines and applications.

3. Data Analysis Platforms: Tools for data analysis and visualization can help developers make sense of biometric data.

Future of Biometrics in Gaming

THE INTEGRATION OF biometrics in games is likely to continue growing. As technology advances and the understanding of player behavior deepens, biometric data can contribute to more engaging and personalized gaming experiences. However, developers must navigate the ethical, privacy, and technical challenges associated with collecting and using biometric information in games.

In summary, biometrics offer exciting possibilities for game developers to create more immersive and adaptive gameplay experiences. By responsibly integrating biometric data, games can become not only more entertaining but also more attuned to the emotions and well-being of the players.

Section 17.3: Brain-computer Interfaces

BRAIN-COMPUTER INTERFACES (BCIs) are a fascinating and rapidly advancing field that holds great potential for gaming and other applications. BCIs enable direct communication between the human brain and external devices, opening up new possibilities for immersive and interactive experiences. In this section, we'll explore the concept of BCIs and how they can be integrated into the world of gaming.

Understanding Brain-computer Interfaces

BCIS ARE SYSTEMS THAT allow users to control and interact with computers or other devices using their brain signals. These signals are typically measured using electroencephalography (EEG), functional magnetic resonance imaging (fMRI), or other neuroimaging techniques. BCIs can detect brain activity related to specific thoughts, emotions, or intentions and translate them into actionable commands.

Applications in Gaming

1. Mind-controlled Gameplay: BCIs can enable players to control characters, objects, or actions within a game simply by thinking about them. For example, a player could move a character by imagining the movement.

2. Emotion-based Gameplay: BCIs can detect a player's emotional state, such as excitement, frustration, or fear, and adjust the game's elements accordingly. This can lead to more dynamic and emotionally engaging gameplay experiences.

3. Accessibility: BCIs have the potential to make gaming more accessible for individuals with physical disabilities who may have difficulty using traditional input devices. They can provide an alternative means of interaction.

Benefits of BCI Integration

1. Immersive Experiences: BCIs can enhance immersion by allowing players to interact with games in a more natural and intuitive way.

2. Inclusivity: BCI technology can make gaming accessible to a broader audience, including individuals with mobility impairments.

3. Adaptive Gameplay: Games can adapt to the player's cognitive and emotional state, offering personalized challenges and experiences.

Challenges and Considerations

1. Signal Quality: EEG and other brain signal measurements can be affected by noise and interference, leading to challenges in accurately detecting brain activity.

2. Training and Calibration: Users often need to undergo training and calibration sessions to improve BCI accuracy and responsiveness.

3. Privacy and Ethical Concerns: BCIs can potentially reveal sensitive information about a user's thoughts and emotions, raising privacy and ethical questions.

Tools and Technologies

DEVELOPERS INTERESTED in incorporating BCIs into games can explore various tools and technologies:

1. EEG Headsets: Consumer-grade EEG headsets, such as the Emotiv Epoc or NeuroSky MindWave, are available for developers to experiment with BCI integration.

2. BCI Software Libraries: There are software libraries and SDKs that provide APIs for interacting with BCIs, making integration into game engines more accessible.

3. Machine Learning: Machine learning algorithms can help interpret and classify brain signals, improving the accuracy of BCI-controlled interactions.

Future Outlook

AS BCI TECHNOLOGY CONTINUES to advance, its potential in gaming and other industries is likely to grow. The ability to create games that respond to a player's thoughts and emotions opens up exciting possibilities for more engaging and personalized experiences. However, developers must address technical challenges and ethical considerations to ensure the responsible and inclusive use of BCIs in gaming.

In conclusion, brain-computer interfaces have the potential to revolutionize the way we play and experience games. By harnessing the power of our thoughts and emotions, BCIs can create more immersive, inclusive, and emotionally resonant gaming experiences.

Section 17.4: Graphics for Advanced Robotics

IN THE REALM OF ROBOTICS, graphics play a vital role in various aspects, from simulation and control to human-robot interaction. This section delves into the significance of graphics in advanced robotics applications and explores how realistic visual rendering contributes to the development and operation of robotic systems.

Simulation and Training

1. Realistic Environments: High-quality graphics enable the creation of realistic virtual environments for simulating robot behavior and testing algorithms. These simulations are essential for training robots to navigate real-world scenarios, such as autonomous vehicles learning to drive safely in different conditions.

2. Sensor Simulation: Graphics are used to simulate the output of various sensors, including cameras, lidar, and radar, allowing developers to fine-tune sensor fusion algorithms and test the robot's perception capabilities.

Human-Robot Interaction

3. Visual Feedback: In human-robot interaction scenarios, realistic graphics provide visual feedback to users. This can enhance the user's understanding of the robot's actions and intentions, fostering trust and ease of interaction.

4. Augmented Reality (AR): AR overlays computer-generated graphics onto the real-world view seen by a robot's camera. This can be used for tasks like teleoperation, where a human remotely controls a robot, seeing its perspective with added graphics for guidance.

Control and Visualization

5. Path Planning and Navigation: Advanced graphics help visualize the robot's planned path and intended actions, aiding developers and operators in verifying and refining control algorithms.

6. Situational Awareness: Realistic graphics provide situational awareness, allowing operators to monitor a robot's surroundings and respond to unexpected situations in teleoperation scenarios.

Challenges and Considerations

1. Real-Time Rendering: Robotics often require real-time graphics rendering to maintain synchronization with robot actions. Achieving high-quality graphics in real time can be computationally demanding.

2. Sensor-Actor Loop: Graphics play a role in the sensor-actor loop of robotics. Delays or inaccuracies in graphics rendering can impact the robot's perception and decision-making, requiring careful synchronization.

Tools and Technologies

DEVELOPERS AND RESEARCHERS working on graphics for advanced robotics can leverage several tools and technologies:

1. Robot Simulation Frameworks: Frameworks like ROS (Robot Operating System) and Gazebo provide simulation capabilities with realistic graphics rendering for testing and developing robot algorithms.

2. Unity and Unreal Engine: Game engines like Unity and Unreal Engine offer powerful graphics capabilities and can be adapted for robotics simulation and visualization.

3. GPU Acceleration: Graphics processing units (GPUs) are

essential for real-time graphics rendering in robotic systems. GPU libraries and parallel computing frameworks can optimize graphics performance.

Future Directions

AS ROBOTICS TECHNOLOGY advances, the role of graphics in robotics will continue to evolve. The integration of AI and machine learning into graphics rendering can lead to more adaptive and context-aware robot behaviors. Additionally, the use of AR and VR in teleoperation and training will become more prevalent, allowing for more intuitive and effective human-robot collaboration.

In conclusion, graphics in advanced robotics are not merely for aesthetic purposes but serve critical functions in simulation, human-robot interaction, control, and visualization. Realistic graphics enable robots to better perceive and interact with their environment, contributing to safer and more capable robotic systems. The synergy between graphics and robotics will play a pivotal role in shaping the future of automation and intelligent machines.

Section 17.5: Evolution of Wearable Tech

WEARABLE TECHNOLOGY has undergone significant evolution over the years, transforming how we interact with digital information and augmenting our daily lives. This section explores the history and development of wearable technology, from early prototypes to the latest innovations, and discusses its impact on various industries.

Historical Perspective

THE CONCEPT OF WEARABLE technology dates back to the 1960s and 70s when rudimentary devices like the calculator watch and early hearing aids emerged. These devices were often bulky and had limited functionality.

1. Digital Watches: Digital watches were among the earliest wearables, offering features like timekeeping and basic calculators. They paved the way for more sophisticated smartwatches.

2. Hearing Aids: Early hearing aids incorporated wearable technology to assist individuals with hearing impairments.

Rise of Smartwatches

THE INTRODUCTION OF the modern smartwatch in the early 2010s marked a turning point in wearable technology. Companies like Apple, Samsung, and Fitbit played a significant role in popularizing this category.

1. Apple Watch: The Apple Watch, first released in 2015, revolutionized the smartwatch market. It offered features like fitness tracking, notifications, and app integration, becoming a health and fitness companion for millions.

2. Fitness Trackers: Wearable fitness trackers, like those from Fitbit, Garmin, and Xiaomi, gained popularity for their ability to monitor physical activity, heart rate, and sleep patterns.

Augmented Reality (AR) and Virtual Reality (VR)

THE DEVELOPMENT OF AR and VR technologies has expanded the possibilities for wearables. AR glasses, like Google Glass and Microsoft HoloLens, overlay digital information on the real world, while VR headsets immerse users in virtual environments.

1. Google Glass: Google Glass, introduced in 2013, was one of the first AR wearables. It offered hands-free access to information and captured images and videos.

2. VR Headsets: Oculus Rift, HTC Vive, and PlayStation VR brought VR experiences to consumers, enabling immersive gaming and virtual exploration.

Healthcare and Biometrics

WEARABLE TECHNOLOGY has made significant inroads in the healthcare sector, allowing for continuous monitoring of vital signs and providing valuable health insights.

1. Health Monitoring: Wearables like the Apple Watch Series 4 and later models include features like ECG (electrocardiogram) and blood oxygen monitoring, enabling users to track their health.

2. Remote Patient Monitoring: Wearable devices are increasingly used for remote patient monitoring, enabling healthcare providers to collect real-time data and improve patient care.

Fashion and Lifestyle

DESIGN AND AESTHETICS have become essential aspects of wearable technology, blurring the lines between fashion and tech.

1. Fashion Tech: Companies like Fossil and Kate Spade have integrated smart technology into stylish accessories, offering smartwatches and hybrid watches.

2. Hearables: Wireless earbuds, often referred to as hearables, combine audio technology with features like voice assistants and fitness tracking.

Future Trends

THE FUTURE OF WEARABLE technology holds exciting possibilities:

1. Healthcare Advancements: Wearables will continue to advance in healthcare, with more accurate sensors and deeper integration with healthcare systems.

2. Extended Reality (XR): XR, encompassing AR, VR, and mixed reality, will create immersive experiences and find applications beyond gaming and entertainment.

3. Wearable AI: AI-driven wearables will offer personalized recommendations, language translation, and enhanced contextual awareness.

4. Flexible Displays: Innovations in flexible and foldable displays will lead to more comfortable and versatile wearable devices.

IN CONCLUSION, WEARABLE technology has evolved from basic gadgets to sophisticated, multifunctional devices that have transformed industries and how we interact with technology. As wearables continue to evolve, they will play an increasingly integral role in our lives, offering new levels of convenience, connectivity, and personalization.

Chapter 18: Open Standards and Future Graphics APIs

Section 18.1: Beyond OpenGL: Vulkan and DirectX

In the realm of computer graphics and game development, graphics APIs (Application Programming Interfaces) are essential tools that allow developers to interact with and utilize the hardware capabilities of GPUs (Graphics Processing Units). OpenGL has been a long-standing and widely used graphics API, but it is important to explore its successors and alternatives to understand the evolving landscape of graphics programming.

The Legacy of OpenGL

OPENGL, SHORT FOR OPEN Graphics Library, was first introduced in the early 1990s and quickly gained popularity as a cross-platform, vendor-agnostic graphics API. It provided a standardized way for developers to create 2D and 3D graphics across various hardware platforms.

OpenGL's Strengths:

- **Cross-Platform Compatibility:** OpenGL's cross-platform nature made it a preferred choice for developers aiming to target multiple operating systems.

- **Community and Ecosystem:** Over the years, OpenGL fostered a robust community of developers, and a wealth of tutorials, documentation, and libraries were created around it.

- **Shader-Based Rendering:** OpenGL introduced programmable shaders, allowing developers to write custom shader code for various stages of the graphics pipeline.

The Emergence of Vulkan

AS GRAPHICS HARDWARE evolved, developers and hardware vendors began to recognize the limitations of OpenGL, particularly in terms of performance and efficiency. Vulkan emerged as a modern and low-level graphics API designed to address these limitations.

Vulkan's Advantages:

- **Explicit Control:** Vulkan offers developers more direct control over the GPU, enabling better optimization and parallelism. This makes it particularly suitable for high-performance applications.

- **Multi-Threading Support:** Vulkan was built with multi-threading in mind, allowing developers to take full advantage of modern CPUs with multiple cores.

- **Reduced Driver Overhead:** By minimizing the driver's role in resource management, Vulkan reduces CPU overhead, leading to improved performance.

DirectX: Microsoft's Graphics API

DIRECTX, DEVELOPED by Microsoft, is a collection of APIs that encompass various aspects of multimedia and game development, with a strong focus on Windows platforms. DirectX includes components like Direct3D for graphics, DirectSound for audio, and DirectInput for input handling.

DirectX's Role:

- **Windows-Centric:** DirectX is primarily tailored for Windows-based systems, making it a natural choice for PC gaming.

- **DirectX 12:** DirectX 12, the latest version of the API, shares some design principles with Vulkan, such as reduced CPU overhead and improved multi-threading support.

Choosing the Right API

THE CHOICE BETWEEN OpenGL, Vulkan, and DirectX depends on several factors, including the target platforms, development resources, and project requirements.

- **Cross-Platform Development:** For cross-platform games or applications, OpenGL and Vulkan are strong contenders.

- **Windows Exclusivity:** If your focus is primarily on Windows, DirectX might provide a more streamlined development experience.

- **Performance Demands:** High-performance applications may benefit from Vulkan or DirectX 12 due to their efficiency and low-level control.

It's important to note that while Vulkan and DirectX 12 offer advantages in terms of performance and efficiency, they also come with greater complexity and a steeper learning curve compared to OpenGL. Therefore, the choice of API should align with the project's goals and the developer's expertise.

In this chapter, we will delve deeper into the capabilities, features, and best practices for using Vulkan and DirectX, exploring how they shape the future of graphics programming and their roles in modern game development.

Section 18.2: Open Standards in the Graphics World

THE WORLD OF COMPUTER graphics has witnessed a significant shift towards open standards in recent years. Open standards are specifications that are publicly available and not controlled by a single entity or organization. They play a crucial role in shaping the future of graphics programming by fostering collaboration, innovation, and cross-platform compatibility.

The Importance of Open Standards

Interoperability and Compatibility

OPEN STANDARDS PROMOTE interoperability, allowing different software and hardware components to work together seamlessly. This is particularly valuable in the graphics domain, where diverse applications and devices need to communicate effectively. Developers can rely on these standards to ensure their software runs on a variety of platforms without major modifications.

Avoiding Vendor Lock-In

CLOSED, PROPRIETARY standards can lead to vendor lock-in, where developers are tied to a specific vendor's technologies. Open standards mitigate this risk by providing alternatives that are not controlled by any single company. This fosters healthy competition, encourages innovation, and gives developers the freedom to choose the best tools for their needs.

Khronos Group: Driving Open Standards

ONE PROMINENT ORGANIZATION driving open standards in the graphics industry is the Khronos Group. Khronos develops and maintains a range of open standards, including OpenGL, Vulkan, and WebGL, which have a significant impact on graphics programming.

OpenGL to Vulkan Transition

KHRONOS GROUP PLAYED a pivotal role in the transition from OpenGL to Vulkan. Vulkan's design principles, emphasizing low-level control and efficiency, align with the industry's evolving needs. This transition demonstrates the organization's commitment to adapting to changing technology landscapes.

WebGL: Bringing 3D Graphics to the Web

WEBGL, ANOTHER KHRONOS standard, enables the integration of 3D graphics into web applications. It provides a JavaScript API for rendering interactive 3D graphics within a web browser without the need for plugins. This has opened up exciting possibilities for web-based games, interactive visualizations, and augmented reality experiences.

The Role of OpenXR in VR/AR

OPENXR IS AN OPEN STANDARD developed by the Khronos Group that aims to standardize interactions with virtual and augmented reality devices, including headsets and controllers. By providing a unified API, OpenXR simplifies VR/AR development, making it easier for developers to create cross-platform experiences.

Cross-API Techniques and Tools

WITH THE ADVENT OF open standards like Vulkan and DirectX, developers have explored cross-API techniques and tools. These solutions aim to provide a common abstraction layer, allowing developers to write code that can target multiple graphics APIs simultaneously. While challenging, this approach can simplify cross-platform development by reducing the need for API-specific code.

The Future Landscape

THE FUTURE OF GRAPHICS programming is closely tied to open standards. As technology evolves, open standards will continue to adapt to meet the demands of emerging hardware and software ecosystems. Developers can expect ongoing innovation, improved compatibility, and an ever-expanding array of tools and libraries that support these open standards.

In the following sections of this chapter, we will delve deeper into the practical aspects of working with open standards like Vulkan and DirectX. This will include best practices, performance optimization techniques, and real-world examples that demonstrate the power and versatility of these standards in modern graphics programming.

Section 18.3: The Evolution of Web Graphics

THE EVOLUTION OF WEB graphics has been a remarkable journey, transforming static web pages into dynamic, visually immersive experiences. This evolution has been driven by advancements in web technologies, graphics APIs, and the demand for richer online content. In this section, we'll explore the key milestones in the evolution of web graphics and the technologies that have shaped it.

Early Web Graphics

IN THE EARLY DAYS OF the web, graphics were primarily limited to static images in formats like JPEG and GIF. These images were embedded in HTML documents using the <img> element. While they added some visual appeal to web pages, interactivity and real-time rendering were largely absent.

The Emergence of Flash

MACROMEDIA FLASH (LATER acquired by Adobe) was a groundbreaking technology that revolutionized web graphics. Flash enabled the creation of interactive animations, games, and multimedia content that could be embedded directly into web pages. It introduced vector graphics, allowing for scalable and resolution-independent visuals.

The Rise of HTML5 and Canvas

THE DECLINE OF FLASH began with the emergence of HTML5 and the <canvas> element. HTML5 brought native support for audio and video playback, reducing the reliance on Flash for multimedia. The <canvas> element provided a 2D drawing context that allowed developers to create dynamic graphics and animations directly within web pages using JavaScript.

WebGL: Bringing 3D Graphics to the Browser

WEBGL, BASED ON THE OpenGL ES standard, brought 3D graphics to the web. It provides a JavaScript API for rendering interactive 3D graphics within web browsers, allowing developers to create games, simulations, and data visualizations that run directly in the browser without plugins.

WebGPU: The Next Frontier

WEBGPU IS AN EMERGING web standard that aims to provide a low-level, high-performance API for modern graphics and computation on the web. It's designed to take full advantage of modern GPUs and multi-core processors, enabling developers to build even more immersive and graphically intensive web applications.

Real-time Ray Tracing on the Web

REAL-TIME RAY TRACING, a technique previously reserved for high-end gaming PCs and workstations, is now making its way to the web. WebGL-based libraries and frameworks are incorporating ray tracing capabilities, allowing developers to create stunning visual effects, reflections, and lighting in web applications.

The Role of WebAssembly

WEBASSEMBLY (WASM) is a binary instruction format designed for secure and efficient execution on web browsers. It enables developers to run high-performance, low-level code, including graphics libraries, directly in the browser. This technology opens up new possibilities for web graphics by allowing developers to leverage existing C/C++ codebases.

Progressive Web Apps (PWAs)

PROGRESSIVE WEB APPS combine the best of web and native app experiences. They can be installed on users' devices and offer offline functionality. PWAs are increasingly incorporating advanced graphics and animations to provide engaging and responsive user experiences.

Conclusion

THE EVOLUTION OF WEB graphics has transformed the way we interact with online content. From static images to immersive 3D experiences, web graphics have come a long way. The continued development of standards like WebGL and WebGPU, along with the adoption of WebAssembly, promises an even more exciting future for web graphics, where the boundary between web and native applications continues to blur. As a result, web developers have a powerful toolkit at their disposal to create visually stunning and interactive online experiences.

Section 18.4: Cross-API Techniques and Tools

CROSS-API TECHNIQUES and tools play a crucial role in modern graphics programming, especially as developers work with multiple graphics APIs like Vulkan, DirectX, OpenGL, and Metal. These tools and techniques help bridge the gap between different APIs, making it easier to develop applications that run on various platforms and devices.

Abstraction Layers

ONE OF THE PRIMARY approaches to working with multiple graphics APIs is the use of abstraction layers. These layers sit between the application code and the underlying graphics APIs, providing a unified interface that can be translated into API-specific commands.

For example, libraries like GLFW and SDL offer cross-platform abstractions for window management and input handling. They allow developers to write code that works across different operating systems and graphics APIs without major modifications.

Graphics Middleware

GRAPHICS MIDDLEWARE libraries provide a higher-level abstraction for graphics operations. They often include features like asset loading, scene management, and physics integration. Middleware simplifies the development process and can abstract away some of the differences between graphics APIs.

Popular graphics middleware includes Unity and Unreal Engine, which allow developers to create games that can be deployed on multiple platforms with varying graphics APIs.

Low-Level API Wrappers

IN SOME CASES, DEVELOPERS may need to work closely with specific graphics APIs while maintaining cross-API compatibility. Low-level API wrappers provide a way to interact with APIs like Vulkan or DirectX through a common interface.

MoltenVK, for example, allows developers to run Vulkan-based applications on macOS and iOS, where Metal is the native graphics API. Similarly, the DirectX to Vulkan translation layer, DXVK, enables DirectX 11 games to run on Linux using Vulkan.

Cross-API Debugging and Profiling

DEBUGGING AND PROFILING tools are essential when working with multiple graphics APIs. These tools help identify performance bottlenecks and issues that may be specific to certain APIs or hardware.

API-agnostic profilers like RenderDoc can capture and analyze frames from various graphics APIs, making it easier to diagnose problems and optimize code. They often support popular APIs such as DirectX, Vulkan, and OpenGL.

Compatibility Testing

CROSS-API DEVELOPMENT requires thorough compatibility testing. Developers need to ensure that their applications run correctly on different platforms and configurations.

Automated testing frameworks and cloud-based services can help simplify the testing process. These tools allow developers to run their applications on various hardware and software combinations to identify compatibility issues.

Code Generation and Abstraction

SOME PROJECTS LEVERAGE code generation and abstraction techniques to maintain cross-API compatibility. Code generators can produce API-specific code from a common source, reducing the need for manual API-specific development.

By abstracting common functionality and generating API-specific code as needed, developers can write more maintainable and portable graphics applications.

Conclusion

CROSS-API TECHNIQUES and tools are essential for graphics developers aiming to reach a wide audience across different platforms and devices. Whether through abstraction layers, middleware, or low-level API wrappers, these tools help bridge the gap between diverse graphics APIs and simplify the development process. When combined with robust debugging, profiling, testing, and code generation practices, developers can ensure their graphics applications run smoothly on a variety of hardware and software configurations.

Section 18.5: The Future Landscape of Graphics Programming

THE FIELD OF GRAPHICS programming is dynamic and continually evolving. As technology advances and new paradigms emerge, it's crucial to anticipate the future landscape of graphics programming to stay ahead of the curve. In this section, we'll explore some of the key trends and developments that may shape the future of graphics programming.

Real-time Ray Tracing

REAL-TIME RAY TRACING has gained significant attention in recent years. With advancements in hardware and APIs like DirectX 12 Ultimate and Vulkan Ray Tracing, real-time ray tracing is becoming more accessible. This technology enables stunning visual effects, including realistic lighting, reflections, and shadows. As hardware support continues to grow, real-time ray tracing is expected to become a standard feature in future graphics applications.

AI and Machine Learning Integration

AI AND MACHINE LEARNING are making their way into graphics programming. From content generation and procedural modeling to adaptive rendering techniques, AI-driven solutions are streamlining the development process and enhancing visual quality. Expect to see more integration of AI and machine learning in graphics tools and libraries.

Quantum Computing

WHILE STILL IN ITS infancy, quantum computing has the potential to revolutionize graphics programming. Quantum computers can handle complex calculations much faster than classical computers, which could lead to significant advancements in rendering, simulation, and optimization. As quantum computing technology matures, it may become a game-changer in the field.

Web-Based Graphics

WEB-BASED GRAPHICS are becoming increasingly sophisticated. Technologies like WebGPU are bridging the gap between web and native graphics programming. This trend enables the development of complex 3D web applications, including games, simulations, and interactive visualizations, directly within web browsers.

AR and VR Integration

AUGMENTED REALITY (AR) and virtual reality (VR) are poised for continued growth. As AR and VR hardware becomes more accessible and powerful, graphics programmers will play a vital role in creating immersive experiences. Expect to see new graphics techniques and tools tailored for AR and VR development.

Cross-Platform Development

CROSS-PLATFORM DEVELOPMENT will remain a top priority. With an ever-expanding range of devices and platforms, graphics programmers must adopt techniques and tools that allow them to develop applications that run seamlessly across different environments. Abstraction layers, middleware, and cross-API solutions will continue to be essential.

Sustainability and Energy Efficiency

AS ENVIRONMENTAL CONCERNS grow, graphics programming will need to address sustainability and energy efficiency. Optimizing rendering techniques and minimizing power consumption will become increasingly important. Graphics programmers will work to strike a balance between visual quality and eco-friendly practices.

Inclusivity and Accessibility

INCLUSIVITY AND ACCESSIBILITY in graphics programming will continue to gain importance. Developers will strive to create applications that are usable by a wide range of users, including those with disabilities. This includes considerations for colorblindness, screen readers, and other accessibility features.

Conclusion

THE FUTURE OF GRAPHICS programming promises exciting developments, driven by technological advancements and evolving user expectations. Real-time ray tracing, AI integration, quantum computing, web-based graphics, AR/VR, cross-platform development, sustainability, inclusivity, and accessibility are some of the key areas that will shape the landscape. Graphics programmers who stay informed about these trends and adapt to new technologies will be well-equipped to create cutting-edge visual experiences and applications. Embracing the future of graphics programming means staying agile and open to innovation in this ever-evolving field.

Chapter 19: Ethics, Accessibility, and Inclusion

In the modern era of technology, ethics, accessibility, and inclusion are paramount considerations in graphics programming. As developers, it's our responsibility to create applications that are not only visually stunning but also considerate of ethical concerns and accessible to everyone. In this chapter, we will delve into the critical aspects of ethics, accessibility, and inclusion in graphics programming.

Section 19.1: Designing for All Users

User-Centered Design

DESIGNING FOR ALL USERS begins with a user-centered approach. This means putting the needs, preferences, and limitations of the end-users at the forefront of the design process. By conducting user research and usability testing, you can gain insights into how different users interact with your graphics applications.

Inclusive User Interfaces

CREATING INCLUSIVE user interfaces involves designing interfaces that are intuitive and navigable for a wide range of users, including those with disabilities. Consider implementing features such as alternative text for images, keyboard navigation, and resizable text to make your applications more inclusive.

Color Considerations

COLOR CHOICES IN GRAPHICS can significantly impact users with color vision deficiencies or other visual impairments. It's essential to ensure that your color schemes are accessible. Use tools and guidelines for creating accessible color palettes and consider providing options for users to customize colors.

Responsive Design

RESPONSIVE DESIGN IS crucial for accessibility, especially in web-based graphics. Ensure that your graphics applications adapt to different screen sizes and orientations. This ensures that users on various devices, including mobile phones and tablets, can comfortably use your applications.

Accessibility Standards

FAMILIARIZE YOURSELF with accessibility standards and guidelines such as WCAG (Web Content Accessibility Guidelines). These standards provide a comprehensive framework for making your graphics applications accessible to individuals with disabilities. Compliance with these standards is essential for reaching a broad audience.

Consider Cognitive Accessibility

COGNITIVE ACCESSIBILITY is often overlooked but equally important. Consider providing clear and concise instructions, avoiding complex language, and providing multiple ways to access information within your graphics applications. This helps users with cognitive impairments or learning disabilities.

Testing and Feedback

REGULARLY TEST YOUR graphics applications with users who have diverse abilities and collect feedback. User testing can reveal issues that may not be apparent during development. It's essential to iterate on your designs based on user feedback to improve accessibility continually.

Legal Compliance

IN MANY REGIONS, THERE are legal requirements for accessibility in software applications. Familiarize yourself with the relevant accessibility laws and regulations in your target markets and ensure your graphics applications comply with them.

Conclusion

DESIGNING GRAPHICS applications with ethics, accessibility, and inclusion in mind is not just a moral imperative but also a strategic advantage. It allows you to reach a broader audience and ensures that your applications are usable by everyone. By following user-centered design principles, adhering to accessibility standards, and considering the needs of all users, you can create graphics applications that are both visually impressive and inclusive. In the ever-evolving landscape of technology, making ethical and inclusive choices is a path toward long-term success.

Section 19.2: Addressing Photosensitive Epilepsy Concerns

GRAPHICS PROGRAMMING must consider the well-being of all users, including those with photosensitive epilepsy. Photosensitive epilepsy is a condition where seizures can be triggered by visual stimuli such as flashing lights or rapidly changing patterns.

In this section, we will explore ways to address photosensitive epilepsy concerns in graphics applications.

Understanding Photosensitive Epilepsy

PHOTOSENSITIVE EPILEPSY is a neurological condition that affects a small percentage of the population. It is characterized by a hypersensitivity to certain visual stimuli, particularly those with high-contrast patterns or rapid flickering. Individuals with this condition are at risk of experiencing seizures when exposed to such stimuli.

Avoiding Flashing Lights

ONE OF THE PRIMARY triggers for photosensitive epilepsy is flashing lights. Graphics applications should avoid using rapidly flashing or strobing effects, especially if they involve high-contrast colors. If flashing lights are essential for your application, consider providing a warning or an option to disable them.

Flicker-Free Animation

ANIMATIONS SHOULD BE designed to be flicker-free. Rapid changes in brightness or contrast can be problematic for individuals with photosensitive epilepsy. Use smooth transitions and avoid abrupt changes in your animations to reduce the risk of triggering seizures.

Testing and Compliance

CONSIDER CONDUCTING photosensitivity testing on your graphics applications. There are guidelines and standards for photosensitivity safety, such as the Harding Flash and Pattern

Analyzer. Testing your application against these standards can help ensure that it is safe for users with photosensitive epilepsy.

User Options

PROVIDING USER OPTIONS to control visual effects is a good practice. Allow users to adjust settings related to animations, flashing lights, or other potentially triggering elements. This empowers individuals to customize their experience and reduce the risk of seizures.

Informative Warnings

IF YOUR GRAPHICS APPLICATION contains content that may pose a risk to individuals with photosensitive epilepsy, consider including a warning or disclaimer at the beginning or in the settings menu. This gives users the opportunity to make an informed decision about whether to proceed.

Educating Designers and Developers

IT'S CRUCIAL TO EDUCATE your design and development teams about photosensitive epilepsy and its implications. Awareness of the condition can lead to more responsible design choices and a greater commitment to user safety.

Monitoring and Updates

EVEN AFTER RELEASE, it's important to monitor your graphics application for any potential photosensitivity issues. If users report problems or if new guidelines emerge, be prepared to release updates that address these concerns promptly.

Legal Requirements

IN SOME REGIONS, THERE may be legal requirements regarding photosensitivity in software applications. Familiarize yourself with the relevant regulations in your target markets and ensure compliance.

Conclusion

ADDRESSING PHOTOSENSITIVE epilepsy concerns in graphics programming is a matter of responsible design and consideration for the well-being of users. By avoiding flashing lights, creating flicker-free animations, conducting photosensitivity testing, providing user options, and offering informative warnings, you can make your graphics applications safer for individuals with photosensitive epilepsy. This commitment to safety and inclusivity is an essential aspect of ethical graphics programming.

Section 19.3: Ethical Considerations in Graphics Technology

GRAPHICS TECHNOLOGY has a significant impact on our lives, entertainment, and various industries. As developers and creators, it's essential to consider the ethical implications of the graphics we produce. In this section, we'll explore some of the ethical considerations that arise in graphics technology.

1. Representation and Diversity

- **Representation Matters:** Graphics often depict people, cultures, and experiences. It's crucial to represent diversity and avoid perpetuating stereotypes. Consider how your graphics portray gender, race, and other identities.

- **Inclusivity:** Ensure that your graphics are inclusive and accessible to people with disabilities. Think about providing alternatives like text descriptions for images and readable fonts.

2. Privacy and Data Security

- **Data Collection:** Graphics applications sometimes collect user data. Be transparent about data collection practices, obtain consent, and protect user data from breaches.

- **Privacy Controls:** Include privacy controls in your graphics applications, allowing users to control what data is shared and with whom.

3. Environmental Impact

- **Energy Efficiency:** Graphics-intensive applications can be energy-consuming, especially on mobile devices. Strive to optimize energy usage and reduce the environmental footprint of your graphics.

- **Sustainable Design:** Consider how your graphics impact the environment throughout their lifecycle, from production to disposal.

4. Digital Rights Management (DRM) and Licensing

- **Respect Copyright:** Ensure that your graphics adhere to copyright laws and licensing agreements. Respect the intellectual property of others.

- **Fair Use:** Understand the concept of fair use in graphics. It allows limited use of copyrighted material for purposes like criticism, commentary, news reporting, and education.

5. Algorithmic Bias and Fairness

- **Bias Awareness:** Algorithms used in graphics, such as AI for character generation, can inherit biases from training data. Be aware of these biases and strive for fairness.

- **Bias Mitigation:** Implement strategies to mitigate bias in your graphics algorithms, such as balanced training data and fairness-aware models.

6. Social and Cultural Sensitivity

- **Context Matters:** Graphics should consider the cultural and social context in which they are used. Avoid content that may be offensive or insensitive.

- **Consult Experts:** If in doubt, consult with experts, especially on sensitive topics like cultural representation or historical accuracy.

7. User Well-being

- **Digital Addiction:** Graphics applications, especially in gaming, can contribute to digital addiction. Promote healthy usage patterns and provide tools for users to manage screen time.

- **Mental Health:** Be mindful of the potential impact of graphics on mental health, including issues like addiction, anxiety, and social isolation.

8. Transparency and Accountability

- **Ethical Guidelines:** Establish clear ethical guidelines for your graphics projects. Encourage your team to adhere to these guidelines throughout development.

- **Accountability:** Acknowledge and take responsibility for any ethical issues that may arise in your graphics projects. Learn from mistakes and make improvements.

INCORPORATING ETHICAL considerations into your graphics technology projects is not just a matter of compliance; it's about creating responsible and meaningful experiences for users and the broader society. Ethics should be an integral part of the design and development process, leading to better, more inclusive graphics technology.

Section 19.4: Open Source and Community Contributions

OPEN SOURCE SOFTWARE and community contributions play a vital role in the world of graphics technology. In this section, we'll explore the significance of open source projects, how they benefit the graphics community, and ways you can contribute.

1. Collaborative Development

OPEN SOURCE GRAPHICS projects often involve collaborative development by a community of developers worldwide. This collaborative approach fosters innovation, accelerates development, and ensures that graphics technology remains cutting-edge.

2. Accessibility

OPEN SOURCE GRAPHICS tools and libraries are accessible to a broader audience, including hobbyists, students, and developers with limited resources. This accessibility democratizes graphics technology, enabling more people to participate and learn.

3. Customization and Flexibility

OPEN SOURCE GRAPHICS projects can be customized to suit specific needs. Developers can modify the source code, add features, and tailor the software for their unique requirements. This flexibility is particularly valuable in niche areas of graphics technology.

4. Learning and Skill Development

CONTRIBUTING TO OPEN source graphics projects is an excellent way to enhance your skills and gain practical experience. You can learn from experienced developers, receive feedback on your work, and collaborate with peers.

5. Community Support

OPEN SOURCE COMMUNITIES are known for their supportive and inclusive nature. You can seek help, share knowledge, and engage in discussions related to graphics technology. Community support can be invaluable when troubleshooting issues or seeking advice.

6. Building a Portfolio

CONTRIBUTING TO OPEN source graphics projects allows you to build a portfolio of work that can be showcased to potential employers or clients. It demonstrates your expertise and commitment to the field.

7. Contributions to Libraries and Tools

OPEN SOURCE GRAPHICS projects often rely on libraries and tools that are also open source. By contributing to these foundational components, you can have a significant impact on the broader graphics ecosystem.

8. Code Quality and Review

PARTICIPATING IN OPEN source projects exposes your code to peer review, which can lead to improved code quality and best practices. It helps maintain a high standard of development.

9. License and Legal Considerations

WHEN CONTRIBUTING TO open source graphics projects, be aware of licensing and legal considerations. Respect the project's chosen license, provide proper attribution, and ensure that your contributions align with the project's goals.

10. Documentation and Communication

EFFECTIVE DOCUMENTATION and communication are essential in open source projects. Contribute not only code but also documentation, tutorials, and clear communication to help others understand and use the graphics technology.

11. Contributing Beyond Code

CONTRIBUTIONS TO OPEN source go beyond code. You can contribute in various ways, including bug reporting, testing, design, documentation, and community engagement. All these contributions are valuable.

12. Recognizing Diversity

OPEN SOURCE COMMUNITIES benefit from diversity in perspectives and experiences. Encourage inclusivity and respect for diverse contributors to create a welcoming environment for all.

13. Sustainability

TO ENSURE THE SUSTAINABILITY of open source graphics projects, consider contributing to project maintenance, fundraising efforts, or providing ongoing support.

In conclusion, open source and community contributions are integral to the advancement of graphics technology. Whether you're a seasoned developer or just starting your journey, getting involved in open source projects can be both personally rewarding and beneficial to the graphics community at large. Your contributions can make a significant impact on the future of graphics technology.

Section 19.5: Ensuring Future Tech is Inclusive

INCLUSIVITY IS A FUNDAMENTAL aspect of designing and developing future graphics technology. As technology continues to advance, it's crucial to ensure that it caters to a diverse and inclusive user base. This section explores the importance of inclusivity in graphics technology and provides insights into how to achieve it.

1. Accessibility Matters

ACCESSIBILITY SHOULD be a top priority when designing graphics applications and experiences. Consider users with disabilities and provide features such as screen readers, voice commands, and alternative input methods. Ensure that your graphics technology can be used by everyone, regardless of their abilities.

2. User-Centered Design

ADOPT A USER-CENTERED design approach by involving diverse user groups in the development process. Gather feedback from individuals with different backgrounds, ages, and abilities to create interfaces and experiences that are intuitive and user-friendly for all.

3. Designing for Diversity

GRAPHICS CONTENT SHOULD be designed to represent and celebrate diversity. This includes creating inclusive characters, environments, and assets that reflect a wide range of cultures, genders, and backgrounds. Avoid stereotypes and biases in your graphics content.

4. Addressing Photosensitive Epilepsy Concerns

PHOTOSENSITIVE EPILEPSY is a condition that can be triggered by certain visual stimuli, such as flashing lights. Take measures to minimize the risk of triggering seizures by adhering to guidelines and best practices for designing safe and visually comfortable graphics.

5. Ethical Considerations

CONSIDER THE ETHICAL implications of your graphics technology. Be mindful of the content you create, and ensure that it aligns with ethical standards and values. Avoid promoting harmful behaviors or ideologies through your graphics.

6. Inclusive Design Tools

DEVELOP AND USE DESIGN tools that support inclusive design practices. These tools can help you check for accessibility issues, simulate different user experiences, and ensure that your graphics are inclusive from the outset.

7. Education and Awareness

PROMOTE EDUCATION AND awareness of inclusivity in the graphics community. Share knowledge about best practices, guidelines, and resources related to inclusive design. Encourage developers and designers to stay informed and make inclusivity a part of their workflow.

8. User Testing

CONDUCT THOROUGH USER testing with a diverse group of participants. Test your graphics technology with users who have different abilities, preferences, and needs. Gather feedback and iterate on your designs based on their input.

9. Inclusive Development Teams

DIVERSITY WITHIN DEVELOPMENT teams is crucial for creating inclusive graphics technology. Ensure that your teams are composed of individuals from various backgrounds and perspectives. This diversity can lead to more inclusive design decisions.

10. Internationalization and Localization

CONSIDER INTERNATIONALIZATION and localization in your graphics technology. Make sure that content can be easily translated into different languages and adapted to various cultural contexts.

11. Community Engagement

ENGAGE WITH THE BROADER graphics community to promote inclusivity. Share your experiences, collaborate on inclusive design projects, and participate in discussions about diversity and accessibility in graphics technology.

12. Feedback Mechanisms

ESTABLISH FEEDBACK mechanisms within your graphics applications or experiences. Allow users to report accessibility issues, provide feedback on inclusivity, and suggest improvements. Act on this feedback to continually enhance your technology.

13. Advocacy for Inclusivity

ADVOCATE FOR INCLUSIVITY within the graphics industry. Support initiatives and organizations that promote diversity and inclusivity in technology. Be an advocate for positive change within your professional network.

In conclusion, ensuring that future graphics technology is inclusive requires a proactive and empathetic approach. By prioritizing accessibility, diversity, and user-centered design, you can contribute to the creation of graphics experiences that are welcoming and meaningful to all users. Inclusivity is not only an ethical imperative but also a key factor in the success and relevance of graphics technology in the years to come.

Chapter 20: Final Project: Building a Graphics Tech Demo

IN THE FINAL CHAPTER of this book, we'll embark on an exciting journey to create a graphics tech demo that integrates multiple advanced techniques discussed throughout the preceding chapters. This hands-on project will allow you to apply your knowledge and showcase your skills in graphics programming. The tech demo will serve as a culmination of your learning and a portfolio piece to demonstrate your expertise in the field.

Section 20.1: Brainstorming Cutting-edge Ideas

BEFORE DIVING INTO the development of the tech demo, it's essential to brainstorm and conceptualize the project's core ideas and objectives. Here are some steps to kickstart your brainstorming process:

1. **Define Your Vision**: Clearly outline the purpose and goals of your tech demo. What message or experience do you want to convey to your audience?
2. **Choose Techniques**: Select the advanced graphics techniques you want to showcase. Consider the chapters of this book and choose the ones that align with your vision.
3. **Target Platform**: Determine the platform for your tech demo. Will it be for PC, console, mobile, VR, AR, or a combination? The choice of platform may influence your technical decisions.
4. **Storytelling**: If your tech demo has a narrative or story, outline it. Think about how graphics can enhance the storytelling experience.
5. **Aesthetics**: Define the visual style and aesthetics you want to achieve. Consider factors like realism, stylization, or a

unique artistic direction.

6. **Interactivity**: Decide on the level of interactivity your tech demo will offer. Will it be a passive experience, an interactive showcase, or a combination?

7. **User Experience**: Consider the user experience and how you can make it engaging and memorable. Think about user interface design, controls, and accessibility.

8. **Technical Challenges**: Anticipate technical challenges that may arise during development. Plan how to overcome them and ensure the smooth execution of your project.

9. **Resources**: Assess the resources you'll need, including hardware, software, assets, and collaborators. Ensure you have everything in place to execute your vision.

10. **Timeline**: Create a project timeline with milestones and deadlines. Be realistic about the time required for each development phase.

11. **Testing and Feedback**: Plan for user testing and feedback collection throughout the development process. Iterate and refine your tech demo based on user input.

12. **Documentation**: Consider how you'll document your project. Comprehensive documentation can help others understand and learn from your work.

13. **Legal and Ethical Considerations**: Be aware of legal and ethical considerations, including copyright, licensing, and any ethical implications of your project's content.

Remember that your tech demo should not only demonstrate technical prowess but also tell a compelling story or offer a unique experience. It's an opportunity to leave a lasting impression on your audience and showcase the potential of cutting-edge graphics technology.

In the next sections, we will delve deeper into the development process, including technical implementation, design considerations, and tips for presenting and showcasing your tech demo. Get ready to turn your creative ideas into a stunning graphics showcase!

Section 20.2: Integrating Multiple Advanced Techniques

IN THIS SECTION, WE will explore how to integrate multiple advanced graphics techniques into your tech demo. The goal is to create a visually stunning and technically impressive showcase that highlights your skills and creativity.

Choosing the Right Techniques

THE FIRST STEP IN INTEGRATING advanced techniques is to carefully select those that align with your tech demo's vision. Consider the following aspects when making your choices:

1. **Relevance to the Story**: Ensure that the chosen techniques enhance the narrative or experience you want to convey. For example, if your demo has a space exploration theme, real-time ray tracing for rendering planetary atmospheres might be appropriate.
2. **Technical Feasibility**: Assess whether your chosen platform and hardware can handle the selected techniques. Some advanced techniques may require significant computational power.
3. **Artistic Direction**: Consider the visual style of your demo. Techniques should complement and enhance the chosen aesthetic, whether it's photorealistic, stylized, or something entirely unique.
4. **Interactivity**: Think about how the techniques will affect

user interactivity. Will they be passive visual enhancements, or will they enable user interaction and exploration?

Implementing Techniques

ONCE YOU'VE CHOSEN your techniques, the next step is their implementation. Depending on your familiarity with the techniques, this may involve a significant amount of research and development. Here are some pointers:

1. **Research and Prototyping**: Before integrating a technique into your demo, research and create prototypes to ensure you understand its requirements and limitations.
2. **Shader Development**: Techniques like ray tracing, advanced lighting, and post-processing effects often involve shader development. Ensure your shaders are optimized for performance.
3. **Asset Creation**: Prepare assets, textures, models, and materials required for the techniques you're implementing. High-quality assets can make a big difference in visual fidelity.
4. **Optimization**: Performance is crucial, especially in real-time demos. Optimize your code and assets to ensure smooth execution on your target platform.
5. **Integration with Engine**: If you're using a game engine or graphics framework, ensure that your techniques are integrated seamlessly into the engine's pipeline.

Creating a Cohesive Experience

WHILE SHOWCASING MULTIPLE techniques, it's essential to maintain a cohesive and immersive experience for the user. Here's how:

1. **Consistent Aesthetics**: Ensure that the visual styles of the integrated techniques are consistent with each other and the overall aesthetic of your demo.
2. **Seamless Transitions**: Smoothly transition between different techniques to avoid jarring visual changes. Consider using transitional effects or animations.
3. **User Guidance**: Guide users through your demo to showcase various techniques. Provide hints or prompts to encourage exploration.
4. **Performance Monitoring**: Implement performance monitoring tools to ensure that your demo runs smoothly on target hardware. Display frame rates and hardware statistics if necessary.
5. **User Feedback**: Collect user feedback to identify any issues or areas for improvement in the integration of techniques. Iterate on your demo based on user input.

By carefully selecting, implementing, and integrating advanced techniques, you can create a tech demo that not only demonstrates your technical skills but also delivers a memorable and captivating experience to your audience. In the next section, we'll explore design considerations for your demo, including user interface and controls.

Section 20.3: Design Considerations for Modern Hardware

IN THIS SECTION, WE will delve into important design considerations when creating a tech demo that aims to showcase the capabilities of modern hardware. As hardware evolves, it presents both opportunities and challenges for developers, and understanding how to harness its power effectively is crucial.

Leveraging the Latest Hardware Features

1. **GPU Features**: Stay updated with the latest features and capabilities of modern GPUs. Take advantage of features like ray tracing, hardware-accelerated AI, and advanced shading techniques to push the boundaries of visual fidelity.

2. **Multi-Core CPUs**: Modern CPUs come equipped with multiple cores. Optimize your code to make efficient use of multi-threading for tasks like physics simulations, AI, and audio processing.

3. **Fast Storage**: SSDs have become the standard for storage in modern systems. Utilize fast loading times and seamless asset streaming to provide a smooth user experience.

4. **High Refresh Rate Displays**: If your target platform supports high-refresh-rate displays, consider optimizing your demo for smooth and responsive gameplay. Higher frame rates can greatly enhance user immersion.

Scalability and Accessibility

1. **Scalability**: Design your tech demo to be scalable across a range of hardware configurations. Provide options for adjusting graphics settings to cater to both high-end and

lower-end systems. Dynamic resolution scaling and quality presets can help achieve this.

2. **Accessibility**: Ensure that your demo is accessible to a wide audience. Implement features such as customizable controls, subtitles, and colorblind-friendly options. Make your demo inclusive and enjoyable for everyone.

Real-time Monitoring and Feedback

1. **Performance Metrics**: Incorporate real-time performance monitoring tools within your tech demo. Display frame rates, VRAM usage, and CPU load to allow users to gauge performance on their systems.

2. **User Feedback**: Create a feedback mechanism within your demo. Encourage users to report issues, bugs, or provide suggestions. User feedback is invaluable for improving the demo post-release.

Future-Proofing Your Demo

1. **Upcoming Technologies**: Stay informed about emerging hardware technologies that may become mainstream in the near future. Prepare your demo to take advantage of these technologies when they become widely available.

2. **Cross-Platform Compatibility**: If possible, design your demo to be compatible with multiple platforms, such as PC, console, and cloud gaming services. This can broaden your audience reach.

Embracing Emerging Trends

1. **Cloud Gaming**: Consider how your tech demo can benefit from cloud gaming services, which leverage remote servers

to deliver high-quality gaming experiences to a variety of devices.

2. **AR and VR**: Explore opportunities for integrating augmented reality (AR) and virtual reality (VR) into your demo, especially if your target hardware supports these technologies.

3. **Machine Learning**: Investigate how machine learning and AI can enhance your demo, whether it's for intelligent NPCs, procedural content generation, or enhancing graphics quality.

BY CAREFULLY CONSIDERING these design aspects, you can create a tech demo that not only showcases the capabilities of modern hardware but also anticipates future trends and technologies. This forward-thinking approach will position your work at the forefront of the industry, garnering attention from both players and fellow developers. In the next section, we will focus on the presentation and showcasing of your tech demo to maximize its impact.

Section 20.4: Presentation and Showcasing

ONCE YOU'VE DEVELOPED a cutting-edge tech demo, it's essential to present and showcase it effectively to your target audience. Whether you're aiming to impress potential investors, attract players, or simply share your work with the community, how you present your tech demo can significantly impact its success.

Creating a Captivating Trailer

1. **Video Trailer**: Start by creating an engaging video trailer. This is often the first impression users will have of your demo. Showcase the most visually stunning and exciting

moments to grab viewers' attention.

2. **Narrative Hook**: Consider crafting a short narrative or story arc within your trailer. A compelling narrative can draw viewers in and make them more emotionally invested in your tech demo.

3. **Music and Sound**: Use high-quality music and sound effects that complement the visuals and evoke the desired emotions. Audio plays a crucial role in creating an immersive experience.

Demos and Playable Teasers

1. **Playable Teasers**: If possible, release a playable teaser or demo of your tech demo. Allowing users to experience a portion of the content firsthand can generate excitement and anticipation.

2. **Beta Testing**: Consider conducting a closed beta test with a select group of users to gather feedback and make improvements before the public release.

Online Presence

1. **Website**: Create a dedicated website or landing page for your tech demo. Provide detailed information, screenshots, and download links. A professional-looking website can instill confidence in potential players or collaborators.

2. **Social Media**: Utilize social media platforms to build hype and engage with your audience. Regular updates, behind-the-scenes content, and interactions with followers can help create a community around your project.

3. **Game Development Forums**: Share your progress and engage with the game development community on platforms like Unity, Unreal Engine, or specialized forums

like Polycount or TIGSource.

Events and Conventions

1. **Game Shows and Conventions**: If possible, showcase your tech demo at gaming events, conventions, or expos. These events provide an opportunity to gather feedback, network, and generate buzz.

2. **Online Streaming**: Reach out to gaming influencers and streamers to play and review your demo on platforms like Twitch and YouTube. Their reach can introduce your project to a broader audience.

Feedback and Iteration

1. **Community Feedback**: Encourage players to provide feedback through surveys, forums, or social media. Listen to their suggestions and make improvements accordingly.

2. **Regular Updates**: Maintain a schedule of regular updates and improvements based on user feedback. This shows dedication to the project's success and keeps players engaged.

Accessibility

1. **Distribution Platforms**: Consider uploading your tech demo to popular game distribution platforms like Steam, Itch.io, or Game Jolt. These platforms offer visibility and ease of access to potential players.

2. **Accessibility Features**: Ensure your demo is accessible to a wide audience. Implement features like customizable controls, subtitles, and colorblind-friendly options.

Collaboration and Networking

1. **Collaborative Efforts**: Collaborate with other developers, artists, or musicians to enhance the quality of your tech demo. Networking within the game development community can lead to valuable partnerships.
2. **Pitching to Investors**: If your goal is to attract investors or publishers, prepare a compelling pitch that highlights the unique features and potential of your tech demo.

BY EFFECTIVELY PRESENTING and showcasing your tech demo, you can maximize its visibility, engagement, and impact. Remember that the gaming industry is highly competitive, so a well-thought-out presentation strategy can make all the difference in achieving your project's goals.

Section 20.5: Reflections and Future Exploration

AS YOU CONCLUDE YOUR journey in creating a graphics tech demo that incorporates cutting-edge techniques, it's essential to reflect on your achievements and consider the paths for future exploration. This final section serves as an opportunity to contemplate the lessons learned, the advancements made, and the possibilities that lie ahead.

Reflecting on Achievements

1. **Technical Milestones**: Review the technical milestones you've achieved during the development of your tech demo. Consider the complex rendering techniques, optimizations, and innovative solutions you've implemented.

2. **Creative Aspects**: Reflect on the creative aspects of your project. What unique visual or interactive elements did you introduce? How did your creativity contribute to the project's appeal?

3. **Challenges Overcome**: Acknowledge the challenges you encountered and overcame throughout the development process. These challenges often lead to significant growth and problem-solving skills.

Lessons Learned

1. **Coding Techniques**: Take note of coding techniques and best practices you've adopted during this project. These skills will undoubtedly be valuable in future endeavors.

2. **Optimization Strategies**: Assess the optimization strategies that proved most effective. Understanding how to balance performance and visual quality is a crucial skill in game development.

3. **Teamwork and Collaboration**: If you collaborated with others, reflect on the teamwork dynamics. What worked well, and what could be improved in future collaborative efforts?

4. **User Experience**: Consider the user experience and how it can be enhanced. User feedback and testing can provide valuable insights for future projects.

Future Exploration

1. **Technology Advancements**: Stay informed about the latest advancements in graphics technology. Technologies like real-time ray tracing, AI-driven rendering, and VR/AR continue to evolve.

2. **Artificial Intelligence**: Explore further applications of

artificial intelligence in graphics, such as procedural content generation, automated animation, and intelligent NPCs.

3. **Cross-platform Development**: Investigate cross-platform development to reach a broader audience. Platforms like consoles, mobile devices, and the web offer unique opportunities.

4. **Emerging Trends**: Keep an eye on emerging trends in the gaming and graphics industry. Trends in gameplay mechanics, storytelling, and player engagement can influence your future projects.

5. **Community Engagement**: Continue engaging with the game development community. Sharing your knowledge and experiences can foster valuable connections and collaborations.

6. **Education and Mentorship**: Consider giving back to the community by mentoring aspiring game developers or contributing to educational resources.

Setting New Goals

1. **Project Goals**: Define your goals for future projects. Are you aiming for a larger, more ambitious game? Are you interested in exploring new genres or art styles?

2. **Skill Development**: Identify areas where you'd like to further develop your skills. This could include mastering specific programming languages, deepening your understanding of graphics algorithms, or improving your project management abilities.

3. **Impact and Innovation**: Reflect on how you can make a meaningful impact on the gaming industry or push the boundaries of innovation in graphics technology.

4. **Passion and Dedication**: Remember that passion and

dedication are driving forces in game development. Pursue projects that genuinely inspire and motivate you.

IN CONCLUSION, THE creation of a graphics tech demo represents a significant achievement in the world of game development. It showcases your technical prowess, creativity, and ability to push the boundaries of what's possible. As you reflect on your accomplishments and consider future exploration, you're poised to continue contributing to the dynamic and ever-evolving field of graphics and gaming.